Michael B. Barry

# COURAGE BOYS, WE ARE WINNING

## An Illustrated History of the 1916 Rising

Andalus Press

Published by Andalus Press
7 Frankfort Avenue, Rathgar, Dublin 6, Ireland
www.andalus.ie
info@andalus.ie

ISBN 978-0-9560383-9-5 

By the same author
*Across Deep Waters, Bridges of Ireland*
*Restoring a Victorian House*
*Through the Cities, the Revolution in Light Rail*
*Homage to al-Andalus, the Rise and Fall of Islamic Spain*
*Tales of the Permanent Way, Stories from the Heart of Ireland's Railways*
*Victorian Dublin Revealed, the Remarkable Legacy of Nineteenth-Century Dublin*
*Fifty Things to do in Dublin*
*Dublin's Strangest Tales (*with Patrick Sammon*)*
*Beyond the Chaos, the Remarkable Heritage of Syria*
*The Green Divide, an Illustrated History of the Irish Civil War*

Jacket Images
Front flap: top image, Mauser C96 – National Library of Ireland; bottom image – author's collection.Front cover: top and bottom middle images – National Library of Ireland; below, Connolly & Pearse images – Risteárd Mulcahy; melange of images of writing – Military Archives, Irish Capuchin Provincial Archives. Back cover: top images, flag – National Museum of Ireland, Volunteers – Pearse Museum; bottom image – Curragh Military Museum. Back flap: top image – author's collection; author photograph – Veronica Barry; bottom image, Allen Library.

End papers
Scene in the GPO – Walter Paget, National Library of Ireland.

Jacket design by Anú Design
Maps and book design by Michael B. Barry
Vignettes at chapter headings by Veronica Barry
Printed by Białostockie Zakłady Graficzne SA, Poland.

The title of the book is taken from a communiqué written by James Connolly in the GPO HQ, addressed to his soldiers, on 28th April 1916. It includes: *"This is the fifth day of the establishment of the Irish Republic...For the first time in 700 years the flag of a free Ireland floats triumphantly in Dublin city...Courage boys, we are winning and in the hour of our victory let us not forget the splendid women who have every way stood by us and cheered us on. Never had a man or woman a grander cause; never was a cause more grandly served."*

# Contents

For my *familia nuclear*: Michael Daniel, Olivia Alexandrine and Veronica

# Acknowledgements

This book benefited from the help, insights and scholarship of many kind people. Thanks are due especially to:

Dr Risteárd Mulcahy; Professor Davis Coakley; Paul O'Brien; Las Fallon; John Kirby; Eamon Murphy; Dr Brian Kirby, Irish Capuchin Provincial Archives; Niall Bergin, Kilmainham Archives; Rosemary King and Brother Brogan, Allen Library; Ray Bateson; David Power, South Dublin Libraries; Commandant Pádraic Kennedy, Captain Claire Mortimer, Lisa Dolan, Adrian Short, Hugh Beckett, Noelle Grothier, David Kelly, Michael Keane, Military Archives, Cathal Brugha Barracks and Conor Dodd and Shane Mac Thomáis (RIP), of Glasnevin Museum.

The following were very helpful to me: Robert Ballagh; James Connolly Heron; Lorcan Collins; Derek Jones; John Liddiard; Cliff Housley; Tony McGettigan; Peter Rigney; Diarmuid O'Connor; Eadaoin Ní Chléirigh; Joe Walsh; Kevin McCaughan; Pat Quigley; David Byrne; Colm Galligan; Gerry O'Mahony, Angus Laverty, Stephen Ferguson, *An Post;* Michael Hinch, *Irish Independent*; Seán Aylward, King's Inns; Ed Penrose, Irish Labour History Society; Robert Magee, RCSI; Colum O'Riordan, Irish Architectural Archive; Brian Crowley, Pearse Museum; Dr Lydia Ferguson, Lorna O'Driscoll, TCD; Marion Casey, Daphne Wolfe, Glucksman Ireland House; Bernie Metcalfe, Glenn Dunne, National Library of Ireland; Richard McCormack, Brian Ellis, National Maritime Museum; Oisín Marsh, Marsh's Library; Sergeant Charles Walsh, Curragh Military Museum; Teresa Whitington, Central Catholic Library; Barbara Cohen-Stratyner, Thomas Lisanti, New York Public Library; Aideen Whitty, Lar Joye, Sandra Heise, Finbarr Connolly, National Museum of Ireland; Lindsay Burgess, Shelbourne Hotel; Ray Glynn, Dublin City Hall; Nick Maxwell, Tommy Graham, *History Ireland*; Clifton Flewitt, Ciaran Cooney, Norman Gamble, Irish Railway Records Society; Chris Cahill, Bill Hurley, Yeka Lomako, American Irish Historical Society; Michael Foight, Villanova University; Karen Johnson, Christian Brothers Province Centre and Dr Mary Clarke, Dr Enda Leaney, Dr Máire Kennedy, Eithne Massey, Dublin City Library & Archive.

Down in the engine room, putting order on my forays into English as well as providing essential and existential support: Veronica Barry and Patrick Sammon.

# Illustration Credits

Images on the specified pages are courtesy of the following (abbreviations for top, bottom, left, middle, right, respectively, are: t, b, l, m, r):

American Irish Historical Society: 12m, 13bl, 18br, 21b, 24bl, 36br; Allen Library: 26bl, 27br, 28br, 30t, 34bl, 55m, 57 pike, 61b, 118br, 123tl, 141bl, 143t, 149m, 118br, 164mm, 183bl, 186t, 189ml, 189mr and image taken by David Power: 61tl; Archiseek: 63bl; Australian National Maritime Museum: 20b; Author's collection: 49t, 86tr, 126b, 137b, 140tm, 140mb, 141bm, 141br, 166t, 166b, 170tl, 170bl, 171b, 195mr; Board of Trinity College: 26t, 88tr, 194t & 195t; carburetor-manual.com: 57bm; Cathal Brugha Barracks, Irish Defence Forces: 85t, 88b, 89t, 145b; Central Catholic Library: 112tr, 159tr,162tl; Christian Brothers Province, Marino: 42b, 122b, 149tl, 198b; Cliff Housley: 104b, 142tl, courtesy David Power; Collection of the New York Public Library for the Performing Arts: 187br; Colm Galligan: 32b, 164ml; David Byrne: 136br; Davis Coakley: 108m, 110t, 111bl, 142tr, 143b; Derek Jones: 43brt, 104t, 158b; Diageo Ireland: 127br, 172b; Diarmuid O'Connor: 22t; Dublin Castle/OPW: 14t, 186m; Dublin City Public Libraries: 77b, 139bl, 185bl, 127br, 172b; Imperial War Museum: 47m; Irish Architectural Archive: 148br; Irish Capuchin Provincial Archives, Dublin: 27bl, 42br, 43brb, 52t, 57bl, 57br, 59b, 61tr, 68t, 74b, 75t, 75b, 78t, 79m, 80m, 82b, 84b, 91bl, 94tr, 98t, 99bl, 105m, 115tr, 123b, 127ml, 130b, 136bl, 137t, 138t, 138bl, 139b (set of 4), 140bl, 141m, 162bl, 167tl, 167tr, 172lt, 172m, 173t, 174bm, 175tl, 175m, 177bl, 177br, 178br, 182bl, 182br; Irish Independent: 58t, 107m, 160 & 161, 168 & 169; 174t; Irish Labour History Society: 73bl; Irish Railway Record Society: 92br, 114t, 115tl, 116b; John Kirby: 49m, 50tm, 50tr, 50m; John Liddiard: 47bl; Joseph McGarrity Collection, Digital Library@Villanova University: 19, 22m, 22b, 36m, 44, 45t, 65m, 162br, 170br, 171t, 171m, 194b; Kilmainham Gaol Archives: 33b, 38tl, 68b, 87tl, 88tl, 119m, 120t, 149b, 159b, 164b, 174bl, 187t, 188b; King's Inns: 175tr, 190 & 191; Las Fallon: 167m, 172tr; Library of Congress: 12b, 14lb, 16 & 17, 21t, 24br, 34bm, 34br, 35b, 36t, 48m; Marsh's Library: 173br, 173bl; Lorcan Collins: 152br; Military Archives, Cathal Brugha Barracks: 23bl, 25t, 29t, 29b, 33bl, 34m, 42tr, 42tl, 44br, 49b, 50tl, 50bl, 51bl, 51br, 52br, 55bl, 55br, 58br, 63t, 63br, 81b, 83br, 94bl, 94br, 99t, 100b, 104m, 106br, 108br, 110m, 111m, 111b, 112b, 113bl, 119t, 119b, 123tr, 126t, 127t, 127bl, 128 & 129, 135bl, 136m, 137m, 145tl, 151t, 179t, 183br, 185t, 187bl, 188tr, 189b, 192bl, 192br, 193mr, 196b, 197bl; Military Museum, Curragh: 33t, 57 all weapons except pike, 76t, 76br; Museum of Technology: 76tml, 76bm, 106ml, 106mr; National Library of Ireland: 13t, 23t, 23b, 24t, 25b, 28tl, 30b, 31t, 33m, 35bl, 45b, 46m, 47t, 51t, 54b, 56b, 64t, 70b, 79bl, 80b, 93m, 97t, 109t,113t, 124 & 125, 133br, 138m, 140t, 140br, 141t, 150t, 153t, 153bl, 153br, 154tr, 155r, 156b, 157bl, 159tl, 162tr, 162m, 167b, 170tr, 188tl, 189t, 193tl, 193tr, 195ml, 195b and NLI images taken by David Power: 28bl, 52bl, 60b, 156; National Maritime Museum: 46t, 46b, 48br, 64m; National Museum of Ireland: 26bm, 27t, 43ml, 43mr, 76bl, 122t, 122b, 162tm; National Print Museum: 55t; Olivia Barry: 18t, 18lb, 20mr, 36bl; Osprey Publishing (illustrations by Peter Dennis): 62, 106b, 121b; Paul O'Brien: 105bl; Pearse Museum/OPW, Rathfarnham: 38tr, 38b, 39m, 39b, 40t, 40b, 41t, 41b, 43t; Ray Bateson: 48b, 50br, 115m, 164mr, 184bl, 185m; Risteárd Mulcahy: 20t, 20ml, 37, 63m, 163tl, 163mr; Robert Ballagh: 31b; Royal College of Surgeons in Ireland: 146ml, 146mr, 146b; Shane Mac Thomáis & Glasnevin Cemetery Museum: 26br, 32b, 43bl; Swedish Army Museum: 47br; Wikimedia Commons: 76tmr – Rama, 130m – www.archive.org/de.

The image on 155r of Pearse surrendering is from an original (small and poor quality) print from the National Library of Ireland and has been restored and enhanced by Michael B. Barry without altering any of the essential detail.

The images on pages 176tl, 176tr, 176bl, 178bl, 182tl, 182tr, 182ml, 182mr, 184tl, 184tr, 184ml, 184mr, 184br, 186bl, 186bl, 192t have been colourised by PhotograFix © 2015, commissioned by Andalus Press. The original images for these (except the image at 184br which is courtesy of the Military Archives) are courtesy of Risteárd Mulcahy. All other photographs and maps not mentioned here are copyright Michael B. Barry © 2015.

The watercolour of the execution scene at Kilmainham, on pages 180 & 181, is by Veronica Barry (who also did the vignettes at chapter headings), and was inspired by a postcard provided by courtesy of the National Museum of Ireland.

Every effort has been made to establish copyright, but if a copyright holder wishes to bring an error to the notice of the publishers, then an appropriate acknowledgement will be made in any subsequent edition.

# Chronology

## Pre-1916

| | |
|---|---|
| **May 1798** | A rebellion flares up, organised by the United Irishmen. It is bloodily suppressed with a death toll of 30,000. |
| **January 1801** | Act of Union comes into force. Irish parliamentarians now attend the United Kingdom parliament in London. |
| **July 1803** | A rebellion by Robert Emmet in Dublin is unsuccessful. Emmet is captured and executed. |
| **1829** | Catholic Relief Act is passed. |
| **1843** | The cancellation of a meeting in Clontarf leads to the collapse of Daniel O'Connell's Repeal Association. |
| **1845-49** | The Great Famine in Ireland. |
| **1848** | Failed uprising by Young Ireland movement. |
| **1858** | James Stephens founds organisation that becomes the Irish Republican Brotherhood. |
| **1866** | First Fenian attack on British Canada. |
| **1867** | Failed Fenian rising in Ireland. |
| **1873** | Home Rule League is founded |
| **1876** | Fenian convicts imprisoned in Western Australia rescued by the *Catalpa*, funded and organised by John Devoy in New York. |
| **1881** | Second Land Act concedes freedoms to tenants. |
| **1882** | Invincibles assassinate Lord Frederick Cavendish and Thomas Henry Burke in the Phoenix Park. |
| **1884** | Gaelic Athletic Association founded. |
| **1886** | A Home Rule Bill is introduced and defeated. |
| **1890** | Charles Stewart Parnell is embroiled in divorce scandal and his power collapses. John Redmond becomes leader of the Irish Parliamentary Party. |
| **1893** | The Second Home Rule Bill is defeated by the House of Lords. |
| **1893** | Gaelic League is founded. |
| **1904** | Foundation of Abbey Theatre. |
| **1912** | The Third Home Rule Bill is introduced. |
| **January 1913** | Ulster Volunteer Force is founded to oppose Home Rule. |
| **September 1913** | The 'Lockout', organised by employers against recognition of James Larkin's ITGWU, begins. Larkin decides to set up the Irish Citizen Army, to defend workers against attack. |
| **November 1913** | Inaugural meeting of Irish Volunteers. |
| **March 1914** | British Army officers, reluctant to act against Loyalists, threaten to resign in the so-called 'Curragh Mutiny'. |
| **April 1914** | Larne gunrunning, with arms imported by the UVF. |
| **May 1914** | An amended Home Rule Bill is passed. |
| **June 1914** | John Redmond's nominees join committee of Irish Volunteers. |
| **July 1914** | 1,500 Mauser rifles, for the Irish Volunteers, landed at Howth and days later at Kilcoole. |
| **August 1914** | Outbreak of war between Britain and Germany. John Redmond soon urges that the Irish Volunteers should fight for Britain. The Irish Volunteers split, and a minority remain. |
| **9th September 1914** | IRB and other separatists meet and agree that it is opportune to stage a rising. |
| **15th September 1914** | Act passed delaying Home Rule until end of war. |
| **October 1914** | Sir Roger Casement travels to Germany to seek German assistance. Early in 1915 an 'Irish Brigade' is set up – recruited from Irish prisoners of war – but it is not a success. |
| **April 1915** | Joseph Plunkett visits Berlin to request support for a rising against British rule. |
| **1st August 1915** | Patrick Pearse delivers an electrifying funeral oration for the Fenian, Jeremiah O'Donovan Rossa. |

## 1916

| | |
|---|---|
| **January** | James Connolly disappears, so as to meet the IRB Military Council at a secluded spot. Agreement is reached on the participation of the Irish Citizen Army in a rising by the Irish Volunteers, already decided on by the IRB Military Council. Connolly joins the Military Council. A date for a rising is agreed: Easter Sunday, 23rd April. |
| **3rd April** | Patrick Pearse issues an order for large-scale manoeuvres for the Irish Volunteers for Easter Sunday. |
| **9th April** | The *Aud* (formerly *Libau*) sets sail from Germany for Ireland with a cargo of 20,000 rifles plus ammunition. |
| **20th April** | The *Aud* arrives off Kerry coast near Fenit. No signals from shore. The U19 submarine arrives off Kerry coast later that night. Does not see the *Aud*. Casement and two companions leave the submarine and go ashore at Banna Strand in small boat, just after midnight. |
| **21st April** | Casement is arrested at McKenna's Fort. After being recognised, he is sent to London where he is imprisoned in the Tower. The *Aud* is intercepted by British warships and escorted towards Queenstown (Cobh). |
| **Saturday 22nd April** | At around 9:30 am, at the entrance to Cork Harbour, Captain Spindler of the *Aud* orders that German colours be raised and the ship be scuttled. Eoin MacNeill, head of the Irish Volunteers, having heard about the planned rising, as well as of the failed arms landing and Casement's arrest, issues a countermanding order, which appears in the following day's *Sunday Independent*. |
| **Sunday 23rd April** | The IRB Military Council meets at Liberty Hall. It reschedules the commencement of the rising to midday on Easter Monday. |
| **Monday 24th April** | The republican leadership assemble at Liberty Hall. Just before midday they, together with a party of around 150, march to the GPO and occupy it. Strategic locations around the city are taken over, including: City Hall and the entrance to Dublin Castle; the Magazine Fort in a failed attempt to blow up the main munitions; Boland's bakery and surrounding areas, including outposts near Mount Street Bridge; St Stephen's Green area; Jacob's biscuit factory; the South Dublin Union; the Four Courts and areas to its north; the Mendicity Institution on the quays. Patrick Pearse reads the Proclamation of the Irish Republic. Lancers making a sortie along Sackville Street are forced to retreat. Troops from Richmond Barracks engage the insurgent positions at the SDU. The British, still with a functioning communication system, send for reinforcements from elsewhere in Ireland and from Britain. |
| **Tuesday 25th April** | City Hall is seized by the British. British machine-gun fire from the Shelbourne rakes the ICA positions in St Stephen's Green and they retreat to the Royal College of Surgeons. The Volunteers have taken over most buildings on Lower Sackville Street. Troops and artillery arrive by train. Martial Law is proclaimed in Dublin. |
| **Wednesday 26th April** | Liberty Hall is shelled by *HMS Helga*, aided by 18-pounders on Tara Street. British troops gather in Trinity College, now a central city bastion. Units of the Sherwood Foresters, recently landed in Kingstown, are decimated as they try to take the Volunteer outposts near Mount Street. After much slaughter, they eventually seize the positions by nightfall. On the quays, after a heavy assault, the defenders of the Mendicity Institution surrender. |
| **Thursday 27th April** | Artillery is taken into position from Trinity College, and begins to shell the Sackville Street positions. In the morning, shells ignite paper rolls at Lower Abbey Street, and a conflagration spreads. As dusk approaches, flames light up the night sky. |
| **Friday 28th April** | General Sir John Maxwell arrives in the early hours. Outposts are abandoned on Sackville Street and Volunteers retreat to the GPO. The GPO comes under direct and heavy shellfire and goes into flames. By evening the republican forces abandon the GPO and establish their HQ in a terrace on Moore Street. |
| **Saturday 29th April** | Conscious of civilian casualties, the republican leadership decide to surrender. Patrick Pearse surrenders to Major-General Lowe on Parnell Street. Around 400 prisoners spend the night on a grassy strip in front of the Rotunda hospital. |
| **Sunday 30th April** | Nurse Elizabeth O'Farrell brings news to the other garrisons, who eventually surrender. The defeated are marched to captivity, mostly to Richmond Barracks. DMP detectives aid in the task of singling out prominent prisoners for trial. The remainder are marched or transported to the Dublin quays and shipped onwards for internment in Britain. |
| **2nd-12th May** | Field General Courts Martial begin with Patrick Pearse, Thomas Clarke and Thomas MacDonagh on 2nd May. Their death sentence is immediately confirmed by General Maxwell and they are shot at dawn the following day. Trials continue in rapid succession, as do the executions: Edward Daly, William Pearse, Michael O'Hanrahan and Joseph Plunkett are shot on 4th May; Seán MacBride on 5th May; Éamonn Ceannt, Seán Heuston, Con Colbert and Michael Mallin on 8th May; Thomas Kent is shot in Cork on 9th May; James Connolly and Seán MacDermott on 12th May. |
| **10th May** | Prime Minister Herbert Asquith visits Dublin. |
| **18th May** | A 'Royal Commission on the Rebellion in Ireland' begins its hearings. At the end of its deliberations it concludes that there was: tolerance of armed militias; a failure of the intelligence system and the Irish system of government was not fit for purpose, whether in times of quiet or crisis. |
| **End May** | Military Court of Inquiry into North King Street killings opens – the conclusion is that no direct responsibilty could be attributed to any British soldier. The military trial of Captain Bowen-Colthurst starts a week later – he is deemed insane and is sent to Broadmoor Criminal Lunatic Asylum. |
| **June** | Sir Roger Casement is put on trial for treason. He is found guilty and sentenced to death. On 11th July he is informed that he is stripped of his knighthood. Casement's appeal against the sentence, on 17th July, is not successful and he is hanged on 3rd August. |

# Introduction

The 1916 Rising in Dublin was a small insurrection. Around 1,500 insurgents participated, although many times this number of British troops flooded the city to suppress it. The total killed (rebels, civilians and Crown forces) was fewer than 500. This was an minute fraction of the deaths simultaneously taking place in the trenches of France and Belgium. As for the Germans (the 'gallant allies in Europe' according to the Proclamation), the Rising did not afford them any advantage in the war, not that they had any great expectations of such.

However, this small revolution in this small country had repercussions that echoed down the decades. The fundamental result was to lay the foundation stone for Irish independence. The Rising led to Ireland's being the first country to break away from the British Empire, after the American Revolution nearly a century and a half previously. By showing that a people within an empire could strike for their independence, this Dublin upheaval proved an inspiration for the process of decolonisation. Together with the later War of Independence (1920-21) it helped to inspire nationalists in India (who used 'England's Need is India's Opportunity', adapted from the original Irish adage) and aspiring peoples across the world.

A myriad of books on the 1916 Rising has been written; as the centenary approaches there will be a deluge. The technique of employing well-chosen images and extensive and informative captions has been successful in my previous books. So, in this book I present the story of 1916 in the same manner. Within the limitations of the caption format, I have tried to incorporate the nuances and twists of this complex story as precisely and accurately as possible. My intention is that this book should be accessible and comprehensive – that someone reading it will gain a clear understanding of the main elements of the 1916 story, from A to Z. There is a host of textual books giving much detail, some written elegantly and well, but many others caught up in the opaqueness that can affect some academic output (see page 201 in the Bibliography, for a select number of books that I have recommended, worthy of initial reading.).

In chapter one, I give context to Easter Week; the origins of the desire for an independent Ireland and the continuity of the separatist movement, so strongly manifested over the preceding centuries. I have split the overall story of Easter Week into two chapters (chapters two and three) recounting the story of each garrison in sequence over those days. Chapter four (post-Easter Week) has several strands. It shows the physical damage inflicted on Dublin by the end of the week. It also details the executions, which caused irrevocable moral damage to Britain's objective of a peaceful Ireland within the United Kingdom. The chapter ends by touching on the complex ways that 1916 has been remembered. It is a topic that cuts to the heart of the present 26-county Republic and intersects with its founding facts and myths.

Few photographs were taken during Easter Week itself – presenting difficulties for an illustrated book. Organisers of a secret rising do not usually have a publicity department, much less 'embedded' photographers. However they were keenly aware of the need to promulgate their message, and made significant efforts to broadcast the news of the Rising via the new medium of radio, by resuscitating the equipment at the Irish School of Wireless in central Dublin (unfortunately, it may be that this message was only received by a British warship at Kingstown). Most available images are of British soldiers posing at barricades and numerous photographs of damage – with one valuable exception, two photographs of Volunteers in the GPO, taken by a photographic chemist, who chose to stay with the republican forces. I endeavoured to add to the available stock of material by sourcing sketches and drawings of action. Also included are a host of relevant documents and a comprehensive series of maps that I have prepared to assist understanding of the action in the various Dublin outposts. Finally, using a technique that worked well in my book *The Green Divide* dealing with the Irish Civil War (1922-23), I include present-day photographs of areas where key actions occurred. Many of these were taken from difficult-to-access places like the roofs of the Shelbourne Hotel and City Hall.

Even though there is no extant document outlining a military plan, the republican leaders (at core the Military Council of the IRB) did have a coherent strategy and plan. They intended to seize positions across the city at all strategic points. While there has been some argument about the non-seizure of positions like Trinity College and Dublin Castle, military historians generally agree that the overall planning was sound. The simple fact is that on Easter Monday, the republican forces did not have enough men. They were thinly spread in the positions they actually held, apart from a few positions like Jacob's factory, where, as it happened, they spent the week with little to do. The rebels were certainly adept at occupying advantageous positions in built-up areas. Small numbers of men held off large numbers of British troops. Without the disaster of the failed arms landing and particularly the confusion of the countermanding order, they would have had a much fuller complement in Dublin. Probably the action in the country would have been more effective. It might have taken longer to swamp a country rebellion had correct tactics of guerrilla warfare been applied, with better coordination and adequate weaponry. The events at Ashbourne demonstrated the effectiveness of what was a prototype of a 'flying column'.

Crucially, the republican forces did not have artillery or machine guns. Interestingly, Connolly is attributed with saying that the British, being capitalists, would not shell and destroy buildings – but they did. Connolly and some of the Volunteer cadre had imparted good training on fighting in built-up areas. However, British troops and their leadership soon proved adept at adapting to this new discipline of fighting in a city. They reacted quickly; early in the week they astutely threw cordons around the city. By virtue of luck, they still had good telephonic and wireless communications, allowing an immediate request for huge quantities of troops, who were easily funnelled into Dublin by rail, and from Britain by sea. Later the innovative use of improvised armoured cars allowed them to progress along streets, despite sniper fire. The use of machine guns gave them a significant advantage. In the final stages of the fighting in Sackville Street, the ruthless use of artillery was the game changer. A failure on the British side was the prevailing 'storm the trenches' attitude, which caused them needless casualties in the Mount Street Bridge area.

In the end, given the absence of hoped-for German troops (difficult to transport to Ireland, due to the Royal Navy's mastery of the seas, as the Germans had well recognised) and the lack of a significant guerrilla campaign in the countryside, the republican forces could not have won. Even had a full complement of Volunteers mustered in Dublin, the British would have thrown more resources into the battle and eventually swamped the insurrection. Given the limited forces and weaponry available, what the republican forces achieved by occupying positions in Dublin for a week was an impressive achievement, and would have been even for a regular army.

The republican forces, a collection of poets, writers and ordinary men, fought, on the whole, in line with the principles of the Proclamation, a brave and honourable fight. These unpaid volunteers fought with nobility for aspirational principles, for no material gain, in a scenario full of mortal risk. In turn, the average British soldier, mostly young and untrained, did what he was ordered to do. Many, particularly at Mount Street, City Hall and the SDU areas, made brave assaults. The British Army let itself down with the atrocities in North King Street and in its attempt to cover up the murders there as well as those at Portobello Barracks.

Military dispatch and a military view of the world led to the colossal mistake by General Maxwell (although being clever and not the mono-dimensional man often described) in executing the republican leadership. From a military point of view, shooting 15 would be a normal consequence for leading a 'treasonous uprising', in time of war (3,000 British troops were executed over the course of WW I). It was the absence of any real control by the pusillanimous Prime Minister Asquith, who should have been sensitive to the political consequences in Ireland, that left Maxwell to follow his own military logic. Even the self-important Viceroy, Lord Wimbourne, so removed from the local populace, was perceptive enough to protest at the executions.

The reaction quickly followed. Public sympathy led to significant support for Sinn Féin, now, with 1916 veterans in the leadership by 1917, taking a more republican direction. They won a majority in the 1918 general election, leading to the establishment of the First Dáil. It ratified the earlier Proclamation of the Irish Republic of Easter 1916. Following treaty negotiations in 1921, dominion status for 26 counties was achieved in 1922 and the Civil War ensued. The pro-Treaty side prevailed and the Irish Free State was established. Republic status (for the 26 counties) was declared in 1949.

An article, which has been largely disregarded in history, was published in the *Irish War News,* issued on the Tuesday of the Rising (Appendix 1, page 199). I find the article (written before Easter Week) to be, in its understated and wry way, as good an argument for a rising as any other. It draws on a recent article in the *New Statesman* which sets out a picture of an England under German rule, on the assumption that the Germans won the war. Such a 'horrendous' scenario is illustrated in every aspect of life, right up to the sending of English MPs to attend the Reichstag. The *Irish War News* writer points out, with humorous irony, how almost every detail fits the case of Ireland at that time. The writer shows that Ireland, living in the half-light of membership of the United Kingdom, but in reality being a neo-colony, was having the essence of its nationhood leached out of it. Irish participation in the Empire including through the army, pro-consulships, Indian Civil Service for the middle classes and education about the greatness of the Empire, created the descent into a mind-set where the Empire knew best. Any concept of an independent nation called Ireland was an aberration. The *New Statesman* article had depicted a situation that would pertain in England after its defeat by Germany, where they would have been "a nation of slaves, even though every slave in the country had a chicken in his pot and a golden dish to serve it on". The sharp shock of the Rising began the process of ending the transformation of Ireland into this kind of Home Counties-type province, at least for the 26 counties. (The partition of Ireland and its peaceful resolution is still an unfinished project.)

Remembering 1916 has been difficult in Ireland. It is the essential founding myth of the State. There are complications in commemorating a vanguard of republicans who were willing to use force, particularly in the light of the conflict in the north which ignited in 1969. No doubt the centenary year will bring revisionism on all sides, as many try to stretch the legacy, meaning and reality of 1916 as a justification for their own current agenda.

The Proclamation of an Irish Republic was clear and inspirational. It was progressive for its time. The element, probably written by James Connolly, encapsulating what the state should be, includes "its resolve to pursue the happiness and prosperity of the whole nation and all of its parts, cherishing all of the children of the nation equally". The part which states: "We declare the right of the people of Ireland to the ownership of Ireland, and to the unfettered control of Irish destinies, to be sovereign and indefeasible" is laudable and appropriate for its time. However, whether we like it or not, we now live in a more complicated globalised world. Ireland is one of the most inter-dependent countries in the world, sensitive to every chill in the world economy. We are independent, but we have had to sign Faustian pacts, not least our dependence on multinationals, and we do not nor ever will have "unfettered control of Irish destinies".

On the last day at the GPO, as British bullets and shells flew, Connolly wrote: "Courage boys, we are winning". In reality, he and his comrades did win. We have independence and freedom from the Empire. However, it would be good, if, set against the framework of the Proclamation of the Republic and the 1919 Democratic Programme of the First Dáil, there were an informed and rational debate on what kind of modern state we should aspire to and how to achieve it.

*Michael B. Barry: Dublin, July 2015.*

*Chapter 1*

# The Genesis of the Rising

*By the 1700s, Ireland, subjugated, had become the perfect colony under the British Crown: a place where the Anglo-Irish gentry could peacefully enjoy their estates and attend their Parliament in Dublin. However, the recent French Revolution inspired the United Irishmen, who sought a separate free republic. The bloody rising of 1798 struck fear in the ruling elite and the Act of Union was enacted to unite Ireland to Britain and its Parliament. Catholic Emancipation in 1829 unleashed a rising Catholic tide. Just after the Famine devastated Ireland, there was an unsuccessful rebellion by the Young Irelanders (1848). It was followed by the emergence of the secret IRB seeking a republic by force of arms. Riven with spies, their rising of 1867 failed. Militancy took a back seat as parliamentarianism flourished under Parnell, but his Home Rule proposal was defeated. At the turn of the 20th century there was a growing awareness of Irish culture and language. The third Home Rule Bill was introduced in 1912. The Unionists objected and the following year the UVF was formed to prevent Home Rule – the Irish Volunteers were formed in response. As the Great War broke out John Redmond offered the services of the Volunteers. The remaining minority, now under effective IRB control, prepared for a rising: it was 'Ireland's opportunity'. An arms shipment from Germany failed; the head of the Irish Volunteers countermanded an uprising planned for Easter Sunday 1916.*

*The void left by the departure of the Irish aristocracy in 1607 (the 'Flight of the Earls') was filled by a new Protestant ascendancy. Left: tapestry of the Battle of the Boyne, House of Lords, College Green, Dublin. King William's victory in 1690 over King James, (rival claimants to the thrones of England, Scotland and Ireland) consolidated English control over Ireland. Large estates and high agricultural prices meant that wealth abounded; many built townhouses in Dublin, which blossomed in the 18th century, and soon became the second city of the Empire.*

*Left: the House of Commons in College Green, which represented the Anglo-Irish in Ireland. Meanwhile Catholics had to endure the Penal Laws.*

*The Society of the United Irishmen, founded in Belfast in 1791, wished to free Ireland, embracing Catholic, Protestant and Dissenter. The United Irishmen were inspired by the French Revolution that started in 1789, and its ideas of 'liberté, fraternité, égalité.' They enlisted the help of the French. The Gillray cartoon (left), shows the French invasion fleet near Bantry Bay in 1796. Beset by a storm, it could not land.*

*One of the United Irish leaders, Dublin barrister Wolfe Tone, had gone to France to enlist the help of the French, at war with Britain since 1793. He had been on the ill-fated expedition to Bantry Bay. Right: Wolfe Tone is depicted here meeting with Napoleon Bonaparte in late 1797 to discuss an invasion of Ireland. Each of the subsequent French expeditions to Ireland failed.*

*In May 1798 the rebellion of the United Irishmen flared across the eastern part of the country like a forest fire. It was bloodily put down by the forces of the state. Atrocities abounded on both sides and the death toll reached 30,000.*

*Pikes against muskets. Plaque (right) of the 1798 rebellion at grave of Tom Keogh (d. 1922) at Knockananna in Wicklow.*

*Below, far right: coffins of Henry and John Sheares in a crypt of St Michan's Church, Dublin. These leaders of the United Irishmen were sentenced to death and then executed in Dublin's Newgate Prison.*

*Tone sailed to Ireland with a French fleet in October 1798. Captured by the British, Tone cut his throat, after being sentenced to death. Near right: Tone's death mask, American Irish Historical Society, New York.*

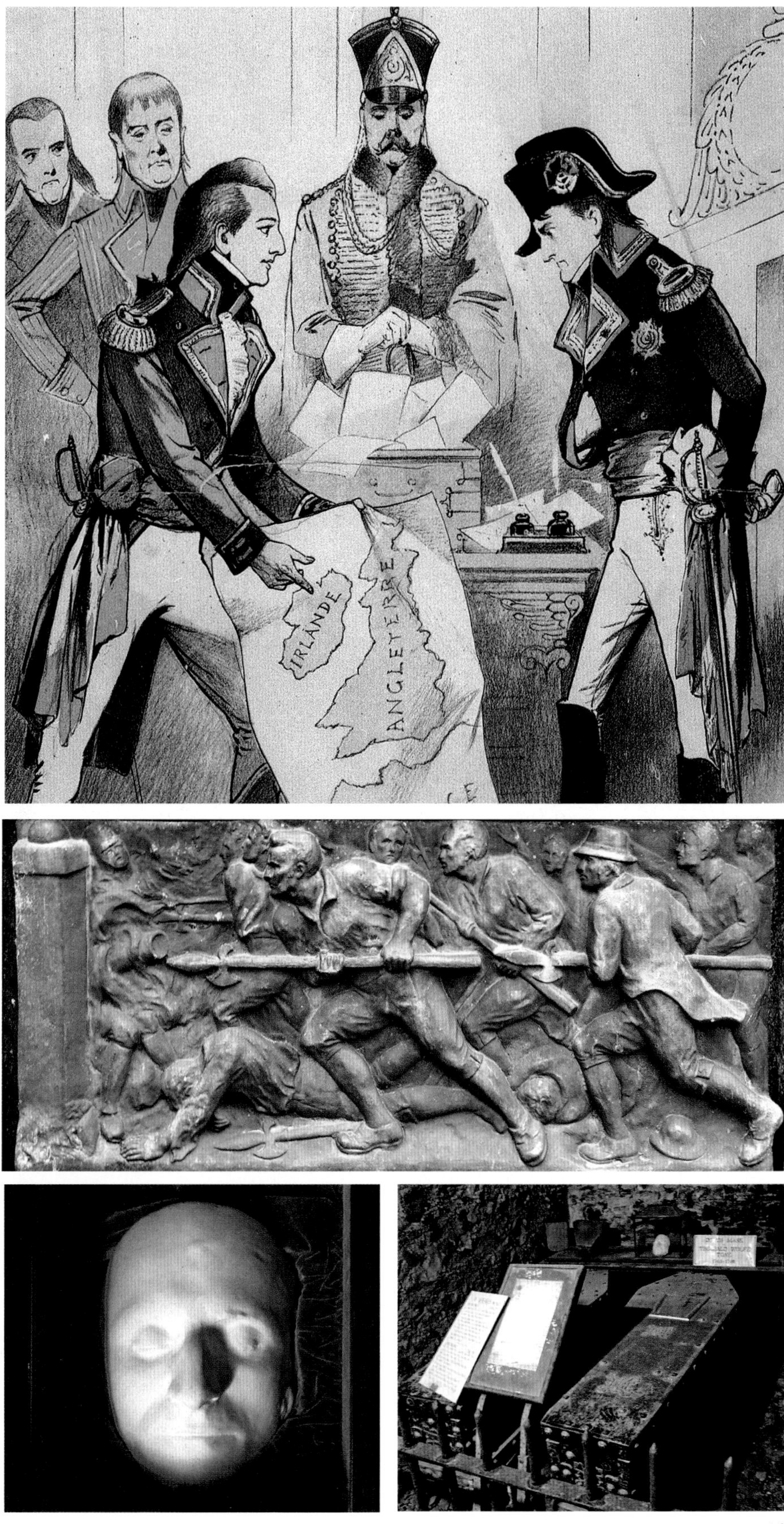

*Frightened by the 1798 rebellion, the British resolved to tighten the control over their dangerous neighbouring island. A campaign began in favour of a more binding union of the two kingdoms. With a substantial amount of inferred favours and bribery, the Anglo-Irish oligarchy in the rotten-borough Irish Parliament was induced to vote itself out of existence. The Act of Union was passed and came into force on 1st January 1801. Irish parliamentarians now sat in London. Left: in Dublin Castle, an allegorical representation, by Vincent Waldré, of King George III receiving from a kneeling Peace the olive branch and the crowns of the kingdoms of Britain and Ireland. He is flanked by Britannia with a flag and Hibernia in a green dress. This peaceful view of the fruits of union actually predates the Act of Union, being commissioned in 1787. Interestingly, in view of recent constitutional tremors in the United Kingdom, this painting was based upon Rubens' 'The Union between England and Scotland'.*

*Left: the rebels had not gone away. Two representations of the leader of the next rebellion, Robert Emmet, who had fled to France after being expelled from Trinity College in May 1798.*

*Robert Emmet, born in Dublin, kept the flame of liberty alive. Only 25, he made plans for a rising in Dublin, with hundreds of insurgents ready to rise up and armouries of pikes and gunpowder. The rebellion of July 1803 proved to be a shambles and failed to capture Dublin Castle. Emmet was captured. At his trial, after being found guilty, he ended his speech with the resonatiing plea: "When my country takes her place among the nations of the earth, then, and not till then, let my epitaph be written".*

*Right: St Catherine's Church, Thomas Street, Dublin, near where Emmet was hanged, drawn and quartered.*

*Below, near right: plaque at St Catherine's Church. It lists rebels hanged after the 1803 rising.*

*Emmet's insurrection in Ireland's capital was hugely inspirational to the IRB leaders and influenced the planning of the 1916 Rising. Far right: Patrick Pearse kept this butcher's block, on which Emmet is said to have been beheaded, in his school at St Enda's.*

*Overleaf: retribution was gory, vengeful and public – a depiction of Emmet's execution.*

*Left: obelisk commemorating Thomas Addis Emmet (Robert's older brother) at St Paul's Chapel, New York. Emmet, legal advisor to the United Irishmen, had been arrested in early 1798. During the 1803 rebellion he was in Paris seeking French help. Granted refuge in New York, he practised at the bar and was appointed New York State Attorney in 1812.*

*Below far left: in perfect Gaelic script, another memorial to a United Irishman at St Paul's. Like Emmet, William James McNeven (1763-1847) was also arrested in 1798. He later went via France to New York and is now regarded as the 'Father of American chemistry'.*

*Below, near left: Kerry-born barrister Daniel O'Connell agitated for the abolition of the Penal Laws. A pioneer of mass democracy, his efforts led to the introduction of the Emancipation Act in 1829. Catholics and Dissenters could now attend parliament. O'Connell then pushed for the repeal of the Act of Union and large meetings were held around the country. O'Connell's refusal to go ahead with a 'Monster Meeting' in Clontarf in 1843 burst the bubble of his Repeal Association and, in time-honoured fashion, it split. He died in Genoa in 1847.*

*The Great Famine occurred in 1845-49 when blight attacked the potato, staple diet of the rural masses. The government of the richest nation on earth, in thrall to the prevailing ideology of laissez-faire, took only half-hearted relief measures. This resulted in one of the greatest catastrophes of the century. Death by starvation and disease, along with emigration, meant that the Irish population fell by one fifth between 1845 and 1851.*

*A militant movement, Young Ireland, took up the mantle of Irish nationalism. It included both Catholics and Protestants, many of them middle class. Inspired by the 1848 Paris revolution, they attempted an insurrection. Forewarned, the Government flooded Dublin with troops. There were some skirmishes in the countryside and the rising collapsed.*

*Right: Fenian engraving. The rapidly-growing Irish presence in the United States resulted in New York being where the Fenian movement emerged in 1858. It was a more muscular manifestation of the struggle for an independent Ireland. The Fenians believed that the British presence had to be removed by force. They grew into a sizeable organisation with branches in Ireland, North America and Britain.*

*'Fenian' is a term that embraced the Fenian movement and the Irish Republican Brotherhood, IRB, who feature strongly in the 1916 story. The Fenians rose in 1867 and were quickly suppressed. There were skirmishes in Tallaght and across the country, as depicted in these engravings of the Tipperary Flying Column ('set up by authority to put down the rebellion'), left.*

*Far left: burnt-out constabulary barracks. After the revolt was ruthlessly suppressed, the Irish Constabulary were allowed to use the prefix 'Royal' by Queen Victoria.*

*Near left: memorial to the Fenians in Calvary Cemetery, New York. The Fenians in the US were at the heart of initiatives against their enemy such as the invasion of Canada in 1866 and the development of a submarine to sink British warships in 1881, all unsuccessful.*

*However, in April 1876, the successful freeing and rescue from Western Australia of transported Fenian convicts further inspired the Fenians' cause. Left: Fenians escape from near Freemantle on a whaleboat for the 'Catalpa', a three-masted whaling barque (purchased by the Fenians) which had set out from Massachusetts a year previously.*

*Ireland chafed under the Union, and the dynamic became a political one for the rest of the 19th century. In 1870, Isaac Butt formed the Home Government Association, whose aim was for Ireland to have an element of self-rule under the British Crown. Right: Charles Stewart Parnell. In the 1880s this Protestant landowner marshalled land agitation and the desire for 'Home Rule' into a formidable political force. His Irish Parliamentary Party promoted the cause of Home Rule in Westminster, adroitly forming alliances with politicians there.*

*The British Prime Minister, Gladstone (seen here, right, in a cartoon, with Parnell – in the reliably anti-Irish US magazine, 'Puck') drafted the first Home Rule Bill in 1886. The possibility of break-up of both Union and Empire was anathema to most members of parliament and the bill was defeated. Ulster Unionism emerged as a growing political force, in alliance with the British Conservative Party.*

*In 1890 Parnell became embroiled in a divorce scandal and his power collapsed. In 1893, Gladstone got a second Home Rule Bill through the Commons. However, it was defeated in the Conservative-dominated Lords.*

*Left: a Gaelic League meeting, 1900. (Note Patrick Pearse, leftmost on fourth row, holding top hat.) At the end of the 19th century there was a strengthening of Irish national consciousness, both cultural and political. The GAA was founded in 1884. The Gaelic League, founded in 1893, espoused restoring (Irish) Gaelic, the Celtic language of Ireland, now known as 'Gaeilge' or simply 'Irish'.*
*WB Yeats and Lady Gregory led the Irish Literary Revival.*

*Left: Joseph McGarrity, an influential nationalist supporter in the US, greets Bulmer Hobson. Hobson, a Quaker, with Denis McCullough, formed the Dungannon Clubs in the north, which were IRB dominated.*

*Bulmer Hobson formed a scouts organisation in Belfast in 1902, called Fianna Éireann. He relocated to Dublin, and with Countess Constance Markievicz refounded Fianna Éireann in 1909. Left: Fianna Éireann Ardfheis, Mansion House, 1913. Countess Markievicz is in the centre, seated.*

*The organisation provided a focus for youth to engage in boy-scout activities, as well as paramilitary training. It was similar to Baden-Powell's boy scouts, but with a republican ethos. One account says that Baden-Powell had made a request to Patrick Pearse to set up a branch of his scouts in Dublin, which, unsurprisingly, did not progress.*

*Right: around late 1913, senior Fianna officers, many of whom featured in the Rising. Included are Con Colbert (seated, right), in charge of the Marrowbone Lane garrison (page 143) and Garry Holohan (standing, left), who saw action at the Magazine Fort (page 91) and in the Church Street area.*

*Right: Fianna members practising field dressing in Dublin.*

*Below: the Fianna Handbook combined practical articles on fieldcraft, with articles on Celtic mythology and the goal of Irish independence.*

*Above: 'No Home Rule' – postcard of the happy nations. John Redmond (far left, on a visit to the Fleet) and his party held the balance of power after 1910. He induced Prime Minister Herbert Asquith to introduce a Home Rule Bill in 1912. Although its provisions amounted to not very much more than the powers of a county council, the Unionist population, predominantly northern, could not accept the concept of even limited rule by those who they judged to be socially and economically inferior, liable to direction by Rome. Dublin-born Sir Edward Carson (near left) emerged to lead the opposition to Home Rule.*

*At first, Unionist opposition to Home Rule was not taken seriously. However, things had changed radically in Belfast since the founding there of the United Irishmen, where Catholic, Protestant and Dissenter had banded together to seek independence for Ireland. In an enormous show of strength, around half a million Unionists assembled across Ulster in September 1912, to sign 'Ulster's Solemn League and Covenant' (example, right) to affirm: "Home Rule would be disastrous; defending... our ...citizenship in the United Kingdom; using all means ...to defeat the present conspiracy to set up a Home Rule Parliament; God will defend the right..."*

*The Ulster Volunteer Force (UVF) was formally established in January 1913. It re-introduced the gun into Ireland at a time when most of nationalist Ireland was focussing on peaceful politics. Paradoxically, the loyalist militiamen were prepared to defy the laws of the Parliament to which they professed loyalty. In support, the leader of the Conservative Party, Arthur Bonar Law declared that they would block Home Rule, "using all means in their power including force".*

## Ulster's
## Solemn League and Covenant.

Being convinced in our consciences that Home Rule would be disastrous to the material well-being of Ulster as well as of the whole of Ireland, subversive of our civil and religious freedom, destructive of our citizenship and perilous to the unity of the Empire, we, whose names are underwritten, men of Ulster, loyal subjects of His Gracious Majesty King George V., humbly relying on the God whom our fathers in days of stress and trial confidently trusted, do hereby pledge ourselves in solemn Covenant throughout this our time of threatened calamity to stand by one another in defending for ourselves and our children our cherished position of equal citizenship in the United Kingdom and in using all means which may be found necessary to defeat the present conspiracy to set up a Home Rule Parliament in Ireland. ¶ And in the event of such a Parliament being forced upon us we further solemnly and mutually pledge ourselves to refuse to recognise its authority. ¶ In sure confidence that God will defend the right we hereto subscribe our names. ¶ And further, we individually declare that we have not already signed this Covenant.

The above was signed by me at Clones
"Ulster Day," Saturday, 28th September, 1912.

God Save the King.

*Right. Carson inspects a Colt Browning machine gun at a UVF rally.*

*Edwardian Dublin was a comfortable place for the middle-class, in their leafy suburbs, but was not so pleasant for the poor, crammed into tenements in the older parts of the city. Capitalism was red in tooth and claw, as manifested when a strike took place in Dublin, organised by the Irish Transport and General Workers Union (ITGWU) leader, James Larkin, seeking union recognition. The industrialist William Martin Murphy responded by a lock-out of the workers and the dispute escalated all over Dublin. Left: the police brutally baton-charge the strikers on 31st August 1913. The strike was not a success and it dragged on into 1914, with the strikers enduring hunger and destitution. Soup kitchens were organised and food was shipped in from Britain. Larkin decided to set up a worker militia, the Irish Citizen Army (ICA), to defend them against the attacks of the police.*

*Far left: ICA men wear a slouch hat (modelled on the Boer Cronje type). Near left: an ICA uniform. Below: the red hand symbol of the ITGWU was worn on the collar.*

*Unlike the UVF (or later the Irish Volunteers) the Irish Citizen Army was not initially driven by constitutional issues but by self defence in the struggle for workers' rights. When the strikers were almost defeated, Larkin went to the United States late in 1914; in his absence, James Connolly was in control of the ICA.*

*Right: the ICA's flag, the Plough and the Stars, one of the most striking of Irish flags, after which Seán O'Casey entitled one of his best-known plays. This example was developed by the Dun Emer arts group and was flown by the ICA in Easter 1916 over William Martin Murphy's Imperial Hotel in Sackville Street.*

*Near right: James Connolly was one of the towering figures of the Easter Rising. He was born in Edinburgh of Irish parents. A socialist, he moved first to Dublin, then, in 1903, to the United States. He spent time in organising labour in the New York area. In 1910 he returned to Ireland where he became second-in-command at the ITGWU.*

EACH FOR ALL. IRISH TRANSPORT AND GENERAL WORKERS UNION. ALL FOR EACH.

"FOR PROGRESS"

JAMES LARKIN,
General Secretary.

Head Offices: LIBERTY HALL,
BERESFORD PLACE, DUBLIN, January 27 1916

Dear Miss Carney

I regret very much to learn about the fire in your premises, and hope the goods of the Union destroyed were not of much significance. I shall try and visit Belfast in the course of the coming week to consult with you about new premises.

Yours truly

James Connolly

*Far right: letter from Connolly to Winifred Carney in Belfast, later to be his secretary during the 1916 Rising.*

*In direct response to the challenge from Ulster, Irish nationalists set up their own militia. The decision was taken at a meeting in Wynn's Hotel (plaque, above) on 11th November 1913, arranged by Bulmer Hobson and The O'Rahilly, attended by many from across the nationalist spectrum. At the inaugural meeting of the Irish Volunteers on 25th November, 1913, at the Rotunda Rink in Dublin, 3,000 men signed up. (Postcard depicting a heroic Volunteer, left). Its objective was to 'secure and maintain the rights and liberties common to all the people of Ireland'. Eoin MacNeill later became Chief of Staff. The IRB secured key roles and control of the Volunteers, de facto, thus harnessing and controlling the forces of the nationalist tide.*

Óglaiġ na hÉireann
Irish Volunteers.
A
PUBLIC MEETING
For the formation of IRISH VOLUNTEERS
and the enrolment of men,
WILL BE HELD IN THE
LARGE CONCERT HALL,
ROTUNDA,
ON
TUESDAY, NOV. 25
At 8 p.m.
EOIN MacNEILL, B.A., will preside
All able-bodied Irishmen will be eligible for enrolment.
GOD SAVE IRELAND.

Óglaiġ na hÉireann
(The Irish Volunteers).
MEMBERSHIP
CARD.

*From far left: poster announcing the inaugural meeting; memorial of the meeting, near the Rotunda; Volunteer membership card (historically, blue had been the 'colour of Ireland', before it was replaced by green).*

*Above: the Tralee Battalion, Kerry Brigade, Irish Volunteers on parade in June 1914. By the end of 1913, national membership numbered 10,000 and increased in 1914.*

*Right: officers of the Irish Volunteers. The officer making notes on the left is Captain Robert Monteith, later to feature as Casement's assistant in Germany and who accompanied him on his fateful journey back to Ireland in April 1916. Thomas MacDonagh is third from the right.*

·U·V·F·

Certificate of Proficiency.

Regiment Tyrone Battalion 5th
Company A Section X
Squad Commander Wm. R. Loughran (FROM WHOM YOU WILL RECEIVE ORDERS FOR PARADE, ETC.)

No. L. 4429 U.V.F.
is hereby certified to be proficient–

(A) In Drill Passed O.C. Company.
(B) In Shooting Passed. O.C. Battalion.
(C) In Signalling Chief of the Staff U.V.F.

COPYRIGHT REGISTERED

GOD SAVE THE KING

WAR OFFICE

The Adjutant General and I have resigned our appointments and our resignations have been accepted by the Government. The issue was a purely personal one, absolutely unconnected with any political consideration whatever. We should not have taken the step if we had not been quite confident that all officers, non-commissioned officers and men would continue to carry out their duties in the same loyal and whole hearted manner which has ever characterised the Army.

I feel confident therefore that I may rely upon you to maintain discipline at the same high standard as heretofore and to allay and remove by your own influence any feeling which may exist in regard to what has recently occurred.

War Office
March 20. 1914

MS 49,178

*Left: a UVF proficiency certificate, fortified by the motto blessing the King.*

*As the Home Rule Bill was about to be passed into law, it appeared that armed resistance in Ulster was likely. Troops were moved to the province as a precautionary measure. Officers who were reluctant to act in Ulster were dealt with clumsily and the 'Curragh Mutiny' occurred in March 1914, centred at the Curragh, the principal army base in Ireland. (No officers actually mutinied, rather, they threatened to resign). In an extraordinary reversal of an army's duty to take its orders from government, the War Secretary John Seely arranged for a document to be issued stating that the army would not be used to enforce Home Rule in Ulster. The Prime Minister, Asquith repudiated the 'peccant paragraphs' of the document. In the aftermath Seely resigned, as did General Sir John French, Chief of the Imperial General Staff (letter, left). The Mutiny affair, which demonstrated the sympathies of much of the British establishment, reverberated throughout the ranks of Irish nationalism.*

*There was sensation on 25th April 1914: the UVF imported – principally through Larne – 25,000 rifles purchased in Germany.*

*Right: events at Larne were well planned – there was a decoy ship and UVF men on duty along principal routes. Carried out at night with elaborate security, it proceeded unhindered by police or armed forces. As news of the event came through, membership of the Irish Volunteers surged, reaching 130,000 by May.*
*John Redmond decided that he should have influence over what was by now an extensive popular nationalist movement across the island. Despite IRB resistance, Redmond was ultimately allowed to place nominees on the committee of the Irish Volunteers in June 1914.*
*Several Anglo-Irish nationalist sympathisers (including Erskine Childers and Sir Roger Casement) met in London to plan the import of arms for the Volunteers. Samples were obtained and an old (and cheap) Mauser rifle was deemed suitable. Then a tug brought 1,500 rifles and ammunition from Hamburg to rendezvous at the Roetigen Lightship off the Belgian Coast. On 12th July 1914 the arms were transshipped to yachts – Childers' 28-ton 'Asgard' and Conor O'Brien's 20-ton 'Kelpie'.*
*Right: Robert Ballagh's depiction of Molly Childers and Mary Spring Rice with rifles and ammunition on board the 'Asgard'.*

*On 26th July 1914, the 'Asgard' sailed into Howth Harbour at 1 pm, with Mary Spring Rice wearing red clothing as the pre-arranged signal. Bulmer Hobson, who made the arrangements, felt that a daylight landing would have a more spectacular effect. In stark contrast to the uncoordinated and ultimately disastrous attempt to land arms on the Kerry coast in April 1916, the yacht and welcoming party were on time, as planned. The Volunteers and Fianna Éireann were there to take the weapons – 900 rifles and 26 boxes, each with 1,000 rounds of ammunition (three boxes had to be dumped into the sea after loading at the Roetigen Lightship, as there was no space) were offloaded at the end of the south pier near the lighthouse, left.*

*Below near left: plaque on Howth south pier commemorating the landing there. A further 600 rifles and ammunition were transferred from the 'Kelpie' to the steam yacht 'Chotah' off the North Wales coast. The guns were landed by smaller boats on Kilcoole beach early on the morning of 2nd August, 1914 and efficiently spirited away. Far left: plaque at Kilcoole, Co. Wicklow.*

*Left: a 'Howth' baton – 200 were made from oak by carpenter members of the IRB.*

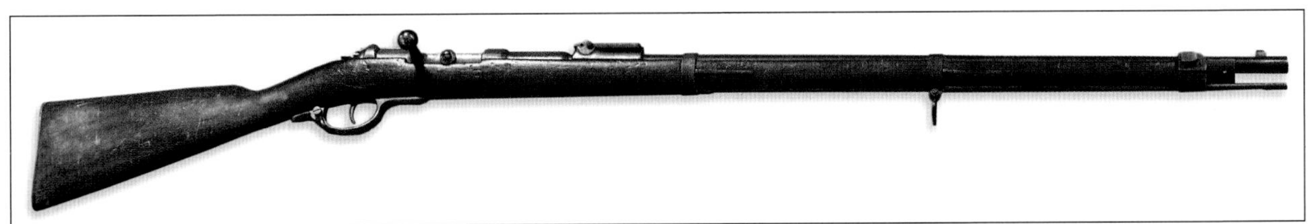

*Above: what the landing was about – an 1871 Mauser.*

*Right: Fianna Éireann members, some wielding batons, transport ammunition and guns in their trek-cart. Most of the guns were carried away by the Volunteers, with ammunition dispatched in taxis. A special tram filled with police headed towards Howth. The King's Own Scottish Borderers, with the DMP, halted the procession at Clontarf. There was a melee but the Volunteers managed to escape with their guns. After marching back, the troops fired on a jeering crowd at Bachelors Walk. Three were killed. Right: funeral of a victim of the shootings.*

*Below: cartoon by Ernest Kavanagh. Neatly lampooning several targets, it shows the Scottish troops and DMP on William Martin Murphy's Howth Tram (Birrell was the Chief Secretary), with the slogan 'Don't forget August 1913' – i.e. the Lockout.*

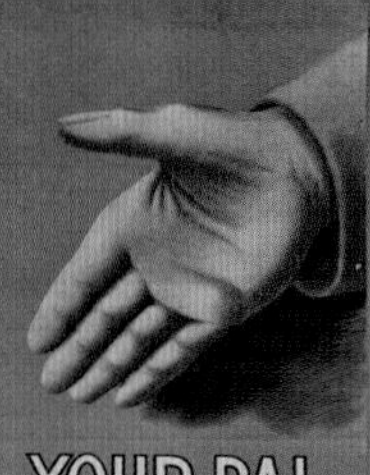

*A state of war came into existence between Britain and Germany on 4th August 1914. Asquith talked of the coming war putting "the whole Irish business... into the shade". John Redmond made a speech in Woodenbridge on 7th August where he said that the Volunteers should fight for the British. The underlying assumption was that, in return, the British would honour their promise to implement Home Rule.*

*Left: the Kavanagh cartoon puts the Volunteers' choice in stark contrast. The Irish Volunteers split. The majority, known as the 'Irish National Volunteers', followed Redmond's advice. A minority, about 12,000, remained, and continued under the designation 'Irish Volunteers'.*

*Clever recruiting posters were printed, left. One witness relates that he saw a recruiting poster in Dublin that said 'Save Catholic Belgium', while just afterwards he saw one, in the north, urging 'Fight Catholic Austria'.*

*After trench warfare became the norm, these training trenches (above) were built at the Curragh, the largest in these islands. As the war progressed Ireland became a support base, a platform for provision of food and men.*

*Right: a recuiting poster urges men to follow Redmond's advice. There was a surge of Irish enlistment in the British Army during the rest of 1914. In 1915 recruitment dropped in response to the horrifying increase in war casualties.*

*Below: this postcard positions the Irish National Volunteers as carrying on the tradition of the Volunteers of 1780.*

# MR. JOHN REDMOND, M.P.

AND

# THE WAR

"I have heard some people speaking of this War as an English, and not an Irish, War. That is absolutely and definitely untrue. . . . The interests of Ireland—the whole of Ireland—are at stake in this War. This War is undertaken in defence of the highest principles of religion and morality and right, and it would be a disgrace for ever to our country, and a reproach to her manhood, and a denial of the lessons of her history, if Young Ireland confined their efforts to remaining at home to defend the shores of Ireland from an unlikely invasion, and shrunk from the duty of proving on the field of battle that gallantry and courage which have distinguished our race all through its history. . . . . Is there a man in this country with the warm blood of an Irishman flowing in his veins—is there an Irishman living with the heart of a free man in his bosom, who is not deeply stirred by the magnificent spectacle of the Connaught Rangers, the Munster Fusiliers, the Dublin Fusiliers, and other Irish Regiments who have been risking everything on the Continent to save your children and your women and your property, and the freedom of your country?"

# IRISHMEN !

Follow Mr. JOHN REDMOND'S advice and join

# AN IRISH REGIMENT TO-DAY

and make yourselves fit to join your gallant countrymen in Belgium.

DAVID ALLEN & SONS, LTD., 40, Great Brunswick Street, Dublin.

*Left: a German depiction of the waters around Britain and Ireland. From the German point of view, support for Irish separatists would help in prising apart the two islands and damage the British war effort.*

*At the beginning of the war, the general mass of Irish people were not against support for Britain's war effort, and there was initial enthusiasm. Around a fifth of the INV joined up, the rest didn't and effectively faded out of politics and activism.*

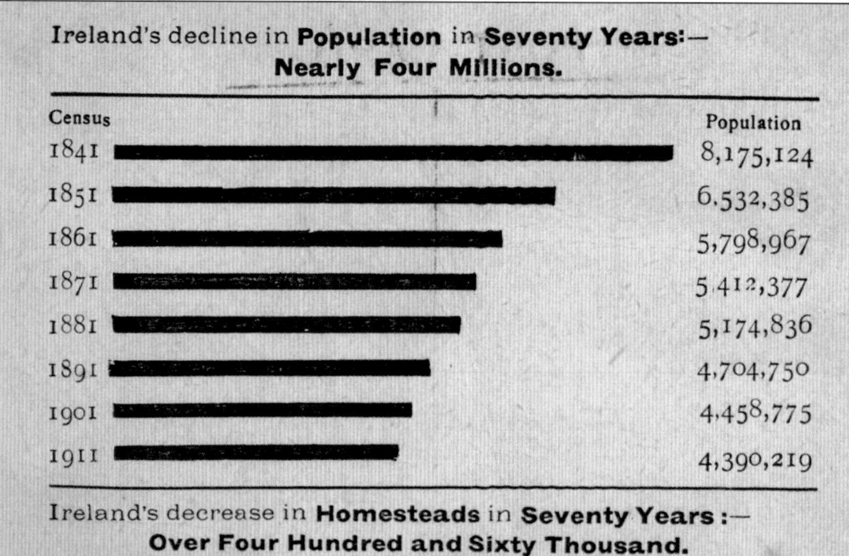

Ireland's decline in **Population** in **Seventy Years:— Nearly Four Millions.**

| Census | Population |
|---|---|
| 1841 | 8,175,124 |
| 1851 | 6,532,385 |
| 1861 | 5,798,967 |
| 1871 | 5,412,377 |
| 1881 | 5,174,836 |
| 1891 | 4,704,750 |
| 1901 | 4,458,775 |
| 1911 | 4,390,219 |

Ireland's decrease in **Homesteads** in **Seventy Years :— Over Four Hundred and Sixty Thousand.**

*One of the underlying rationales for separatism: this postcard, left, in a few simple statistics, shows that Ireland was not just a simple and equal consituent of the United Kingdom. Under British management, the population had nearly halved over 70 years. By contrast, over the same period, Britain's population had more than doubled.*

*Clan na Gael, directed by the Fenian John Devoy (below, near left) provided support for Irish separatism in the USA.*

*Left: IRB insignia at Calvary Cemetery, New York. The IRB had carried the banner for an independent Irish Republic over the decades. A mixture of new and seasoned adherents combined now to propel advanced nationalist Ireland towards insurrection.*

*Right: the IRB were steely protagonists in keeping the dream of Irish independence alive. As well as being a secret oathbound society, the IRB had intertwined family relationships as seen here. Left to right – John Daly, Thomas Clarke and Seán MacDermott. Daly participated in the 1867 Fenian uprising and was active in the United States and Britain, where he had been imprisoned. His nephew was Edward Daly (executed in 1916), whose sister was was Kathleen, wife of veteran Fenian Thomas Clarke. Seán MacDermott was national organiser for the IRB and protégé of Clarke. Both he and Clarke were executed in 1916.*

*Below: plaque at former Gaelic League HQ, Parnell Square. On 9th Septemeber1914, IRB members (including Clarke and MacDermott) met with other separatists here and agreed that a rising would be staged before the end of the 'Great War'.*

*Far left: Thomas Clarke, in front of his shop at the corner of Parnell Street and Upper Sackville Street. Clarke had been active in the Fenian dynamite campaign in Britain and spent 15 years in British gaols. After a time working for Clan na Gael in the USA he returned to Dublin in 1907. Although of a different generation, he had a youthful demeanour and was full of enthusiasm. He proved inspirational to the younger members of the IRB, frustrated at the staid ways of the established leadership.*

*Patrick Pearse, although he came late to militarism, became one of the most important protagonists in the run-up to the 1916 Rising. Above near left: Bust of Pearse by Oliver Sheppard at St Enda's School.*

*Pearse had joined the Gaelic League in 1896. He quickly gained seniority in the movement and travelled around the country officiating at events.*

*Left: Patrick and his brother William, who was a talented sculptor. Below: William's 'Róisín Dubh' inset at the James Clarence Mangan memorial in St Stephen's Green.*

*At 27 Great Brunswick (now appropriately, Pearse) Street, memorial to William and Patrick, above, and fascia, top right. Their English-born father, James, ran his successful stonecarving business here (right, as it was). It was a good time to be a sculptor in Ireland, coinciding with the surge in construction of Catholic churches, post-Catholic Emancipation. Patrick Pearse edited the Gaelic League's journal 'An Claidheamh Soluis' from 1903. He later produced a series of books in Irish. Spending time in Connemara, he bonded with the people there and their language.*
*To provide a distinctly Irish and bilingual education, Pearse founded St Enda's School in 1908, initially in Ranelagh. In 1910 it moved to the more spacious 'Hermitage' in the southern Dublin village of Rathfarnham. This Georgian mansion (right) is situated in 50 landscaped acres, with streams and rocky outcrops. Fascinated by Robert Emmet and his rebellion, he named, in the grounds, a path as 'Emmet's Walk' and a lodge, 'Emmet's Fort'.*

*Above: dormitory, St Enda's*

*A school production of the Passion play, 'Dráma na Páise' was successfully staged in the Abbey in 1911. Left: William Pearse as Pilate.*

*Despite St Enda's being a vibrant and innovative school, it lost money. Pearse was in constant financial difficulty. Under pressure from creditors, he embarked on a fund-raising visit to the United States in early 1914.*

*Right: Pearse's office at St Enda's. Pearse had a fascination with Napoleon, an etching of whom had pride of place over the mantel.*

*This enigmatic poet, one of the founders of the Irish Volunteers, joined the IRB in late 1913. Pearse's reputation as a radical nationalist grew. A proposed meeting in Trinity College, celebrating the birth of Thomas Davis, was banned by the provost, John Pentland Mahaffy, when he heard that 'a man called Pearse' was to be there.*

*Pearse was active in the Irish Volunteers. He was invited to join the Supreme Council of the IRB in 1915. With a reputation as an impressive orator, Pearse was chosen to give the funeral oration at Glasnevin for the old Fenian, Jeremiah O'Donovan Rossa in August 1915. Seeking advice on how his speech should be composed, he consulted Thomas Clarke, who replied "make it as hot as hell". In the event it was an electrifying speech (right, Pearse at funeral). "...they have left us our Fenian dead, and while Ireland holds these graves, Ireland unfree shall never be at peace." It captured the revolutionary fervour of those febrile times and shot Pearse to further prominence in the republican movement.*

C.D. 94/1/4

attack along road No. 1. At e they should endeavour to get into touch with 1st Batt. which will be preparing to attack along road No. 4. This will be difficult, but is important.

4. In the meantime your main body will have moved along route x y p b, and will attack along road No. 2 simultaneously with the attack of cyclists along road No. 1. At b get into touch with cyclists on your left, and with 2nd Batt. on your right.

5. Your cyclists and your main body shd. meet at point marked +c (where Finglas Protestant Church stands). Portion of your force should enter the village by the road marked k and portion by the lane marked m.

6. Point of general rally in Finglas after operation, upper cross road at pump.

P. H. Pearse, Comdt.

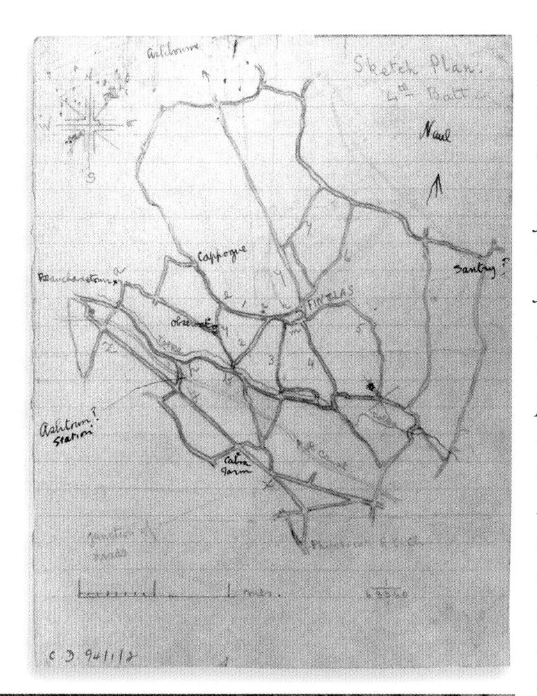


*On occasion, Pearse's prolific writings verged on the mystic. Belying his gentle and introverted manner, he wrote about the sanctifying power of bloodshed in the struggle for Ireland's freedom.*

*Pearse made the transformation from the metaphysical to the practical. By December 1914 he was made Director of Military Organisation of the Irish Volunteers. Left: instruction by Pearse for a large exercise, which was successfully carried out in the Finglas area in Easter 1915, as shown on the sketch map. This excercise in the North Dublin countryside would give good grounding for the fighting that occurred at Ashbourne a year later.*

*The departure of Redmond's Volunteers had given the Irish Volunteers more clarity of purpose. Training proceeded apace (imaginatively depicted, left).*

*Below: veteran nationalist and journalist, Arthur Griffith. His Sinn Féin movement played no direct part in the Volunteers, yet the authorities called them all 'Sinn Féiners'.*

*Right: 'A' Company of the 4th Battalion, Dublin Brigade, Irish Volunteers presents arms in the grounds of the training hall at Larkfield, Kimmage, in September 1915.*

*As the British sank into the morass of war, the maxim 'England's difficulty is Ireland's opportunity' came into sharper focus. Now was the time and the activists of the IRB decided to go ahead with a rising. A Military Council was established to draw up plans and secure arms. The council had essential ingredients: Tom Clarke's gravitas; Seán MacDermott's dedication; Pearse's inspirational energy and Joseph Plunkett's planning.*

*James Connolly 'disappeared' for several days and was cloistered with the Military Council at a house in mid-January 1916. Agreement was reached on an alliance and the locomotive of the ICA was harnessed to the train of the Irish Volunteers. Preparation for insurrection now stepped up a pace and a date was chosen.*

*Near right: Cumann na mBan uniform. This women's republican organisation, founded in 1914, was an auxiliary of the Irish Volunteers. Centre far right: Irish Volunteer uniform.*

*Right: Irish Volunteer belt and badges*

*Left: Sir Roger Casement. Born in 1864, near Dublin, with family roots in the North of Ireland. He worked in the Belgian Congo and brought to light the atrocities being perpetrated there. Now in the British consular service, he served in Brazil. Again, he campaigned against the oppression of the local rubber workers in Putamayo, for which he received a knighthood in 1911. With a growing awareness of his Irish heritage he joined the Gaelic League in 1904. He increasingly embraced the cause of Irishness and freedom. Involved in the formation of the Irish Volunteers, he helped finance the Howth gun-running. In mid-1914, he met with German diplomats in New York to seek support for an Irish rising and travelled to Germany in October that year.*

*Below: Joseph Plunkett, IRB Military Council, went to Berlin in April 1915 to negotiate for support including arms.*

*The Germans were ready to stir unrest in Britain's backyard. They allowed Casement to entice Irish prisoners of war to join an 'Irish Brigade' to fight for Irish independence. The results were poor, with only a handful joining up. Right: members of the brigade at their camp at Limburg, in their specially designed uniforms. Sergeant Daniel Bailey (who used the alias Beverley in Germany) is fourth from the left, beside a German interpreter. He later travelled to Ireland with Casement.*

*Plunkett (with Casement) had requested that German troops should land in Ireland. The Germans were unenthusiastic about sending troops on a 3,000 km journey through seas dominated by the Royal Navy. By now, Casement had been sidelined from the planning in Dublin. He also had become disillusioned with the Germans. The dynamic now came from America. In March 1916 John Devoy informed the Germans of the date of the rebellion. The German Admiralty proposed landing a shipment of arms at Fenit near Tralee, to arrive on 20th April 1916 on the eve of the planned rising.*

*Right: the long looping voyage of the arms ship, the 'Aud', from Germany to Ireland.*

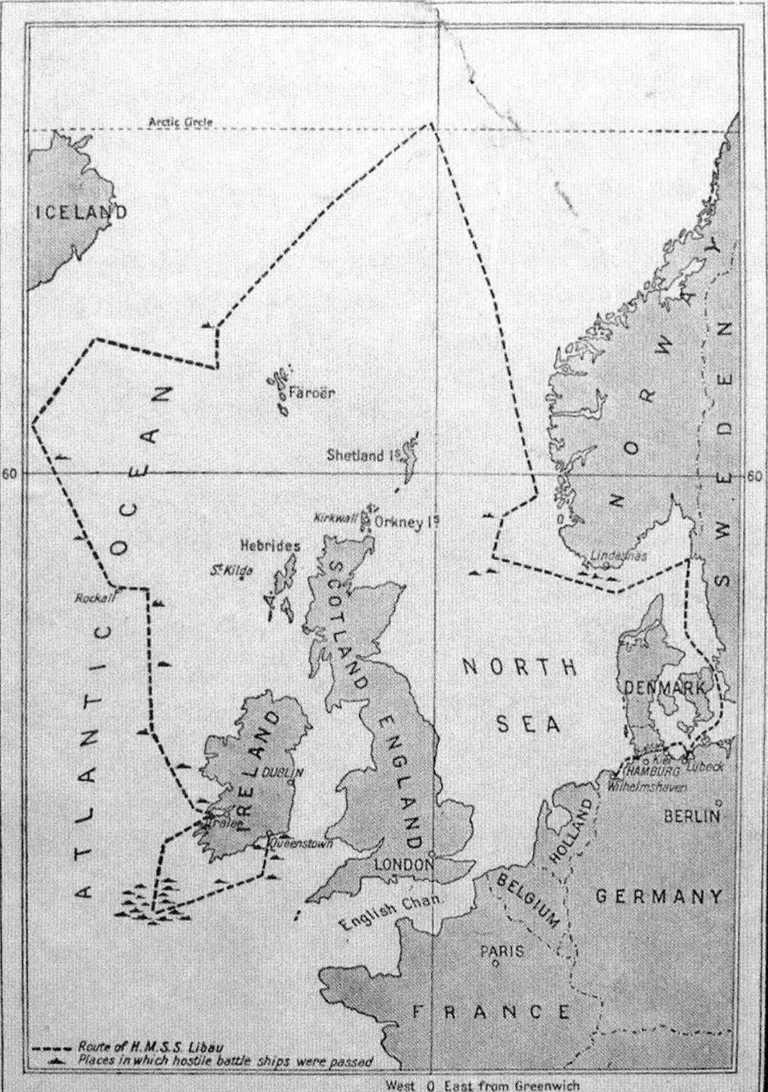

*Left: audacious imposter. The British 'SS Castro' (1,230 tons), had been detained by the Germans at the outbreak of war and renamed the 'Libau'. For the voyage to Ireland it was renamed the 'Aud' (the real 'Aud' was plying the Mediterranean) and fitted out with Norwegian markings and a fake cargo bound for Cardiff and Genoa.*
*After a voyage touching the Arctic Circle, the Aud reached Tralee Bay as scheduled, on 20th April. It moored just off Inishtooskert and gave its pre-arranged green signal. No signal light came from shore. The ship had no wireless and unknown to it, the date had been changed via a message in New York. There was no local Volunteer lookout. The following morning, 'Aud' passed inspection by a naval armed trawler. The 'Aud' headed south-west and was intercepted late on the 21st April by Royal Navy warships and escorted towards Queenstown (now Cobh). 'Room 40', the formidable British naval intelligence division, knew that the arms ship was on the way, following a raid on a German diplomat's office in Washington.*
*Left: on reaching the approaches to Cork Harbour, at around 9:30 am on 22 April 1916, the captain raised the German colours and scuttled the 'Aud.'*

*Right: a dramatic sketch by Fritz Nansen showing the 'Aud's' captain, Lieutenant Karl Spindler, being surrounded by sailors after being hauled aboard 'HMS Bluebell' in Cork Harbour. After interrogation at Scotland Yard, he was interned in Britain and later repatriated in a prisoner exchange.*

*Middle right: the Imperial naval ensign of the 'Aud', now in the Imperial War Museum in London. Naval divers salvaged this soon after the ship sank.*

*Below far right: a Mosin Nagant, the rifle that never was – in Ireland. 20,000 of these Russian rifles (captured after Russian defeats like Tannenburg in 1914) were shipped on the 'Aud'. The rifle was devised in 1891, amalgamating designs by the Russian Captain Mosin and the Belgian brothers Nagant, all influenced by the Mauser. Using a 7.62 mm cartridge (near right, seen at the 'Aud' wreck site), they had a five-round magazine, and, contrary to some accounts, were very effective rifles. It was the standard rifle of the Russian and later the Soviet Army during WW II. Total production, of many variants, was 37 million. Those on the 'Aud' included ones made in Tula, Russia and Orleans, France (made there in 1905 to a Russian order).*

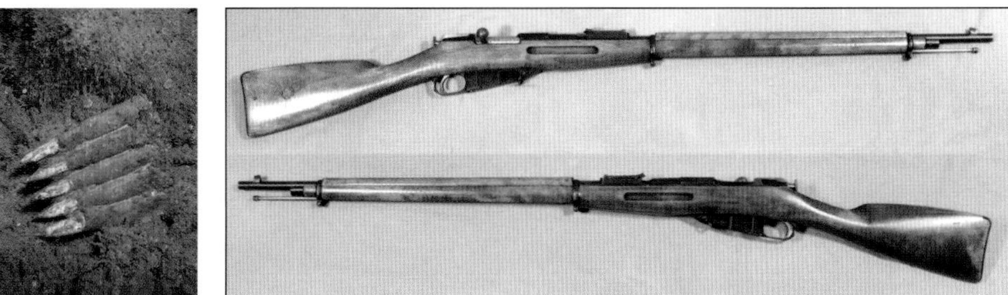

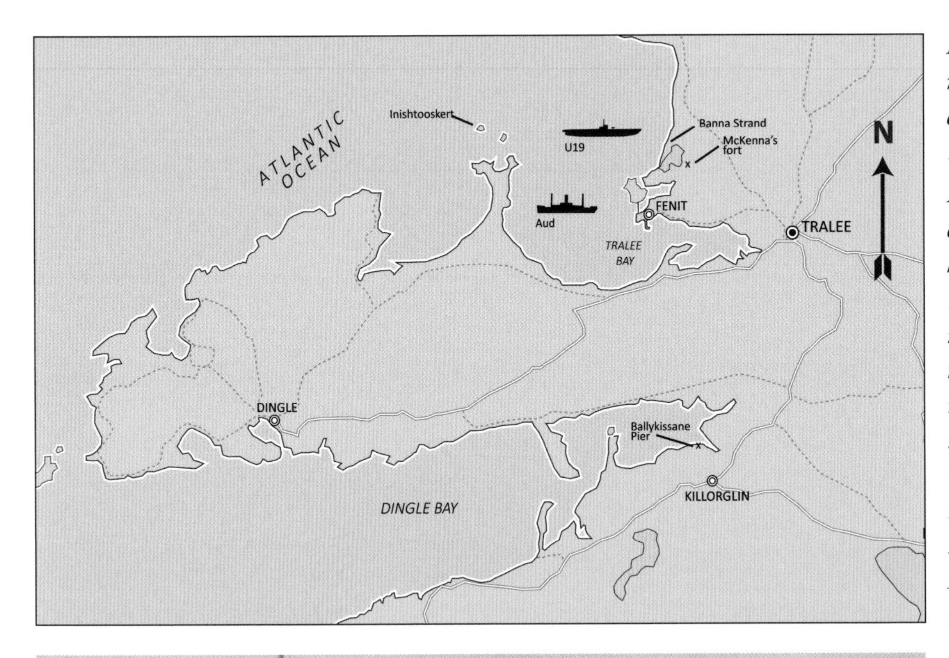


*Left: multiple failures – map showing the Kerry coast and location of the 1916 maritime events.*

*Roger Casement departed on the U20 from Wilhelmshaven on 12th April 1916, destination Kerry. It is likely that Casement intended to stop the planned rebellion as he thought that it would fail; the promised German aid (arms but no troops) was insufficient. His party included Robert Monteith, Irish Volunteer military instructor, who had attempted to train the ill-starred Irish Brigade, along with Sergeant Bailey of the brigade (who later turned King's evidence against Casement). The U20 had engine trouble and they returned and transferred to the U19.*

*Left: 'Unterseeboote' at their base. U20 (the submarine that sank the 'Lusitania') and U19 are in the middle. U19 (650 tons) had been the first German submarine to be equipped with a diesel engine.*

*Below left: deck gun, attributed to the U19, on display at Bangor, Co. Down.*

*Right: postcard of a WW I German U Boat.*

*The U19 arrived in Tralee Bay late on the night of 20th April 1916. There was no sign of the 'Aud'. Weisbach, not wishing to be detected, decided that his passengers should go ashore that night. The submarine's collapsable dinghy was placed in the water, just after 2 am on Good Friday, 21st April.*

*As the Irishmen rowed ashore, heavy waves overturned the boat. They clambered back in and it grounded on a sandbank. They landed at Banna Strand (middle right). An exhausted Casement sheltered in the nearby McKenna's Fort (an early medieval hillfort) as his two companions headed for Tralee, seeking help.*

*Below right: the U19's wooden dinghy, flat-bottomed with canvas hoods fore and aft. A farmer reported sighting this to the RIC, thus alerting them to the landing.*

*Left: pictured on the U19's conning tower en route – from left, Monteith, Bailey with soft hat, officer, Casement (bareheaded) and just in view, Weisbach, the U Boat commander. Weisbach had been torpedo officer on the U20 and fired the fatal torpedo at the 'Lusitania'.*

Preußisch-Hessische Staatseisenbahnen.

Bettkarte Nr. 0113

*Fri* Berlin Stadtb. —
**Wilhelmshaven**

Zug D 6/D 146/D 112/D 122
(ab Friedrichstr. 9³⁰ Nm.)
in der Nacht

vom ........ zum ........

Wagen Nr. ........

Platz Nr. ........

Gültig für ........

I. Klasse. Preis: 10,00 M
Vormerkungsgb. 0,50 M
Zusammen: 10,50 M

Nur gültig in Verbindung mit einem Fahrausweis I. Klasse.

*Near left and above: memorial to Casement at McKenna's Fort. Alerted by news of the abandoned boat, two RIC officers arrested Casement here. He was soon identified (a train sleeper ticket, Berlin to Wilhelmshaven, far left, was found in his overcoat). He was rapidly escorted to London, arriving on Easter Sunday, 23rd April 1916, and placed in the Tower of London on 25th April.*

*The final part of these poorly planned and coordinated events occurred here at Ballykissane pier (left). On Good Friday evening, Volunteers from Dublin were travelling in two cars to Caherciveen to seize equipment from the wireless college there, planning to use it to communicate with the arms ship and submarine. The driver of the second car missed the turn at Killorglin and drove off the pier. Three Volunteers were drowned.*

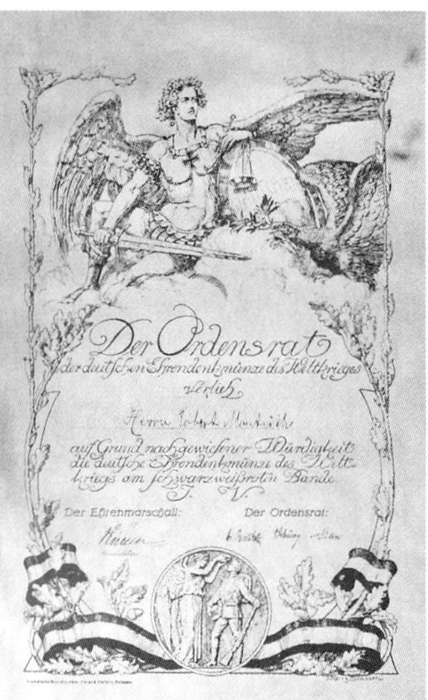

*Near left: mural on Belfast gable commemorating the dead Volunteers.*

*Far left: German encomium awarded to Robert Monteith. He evaded capture and escaped to the United States. Daniel Bailey was arrested and was tried along with Casement.*

*Meanwhile, in Dublin, pre-Easter Week, tension was building up. On Wednesday, 19th April an alderman read out the 'Castle Document' (as summarised by the circular, right) at a meeting of Dublin Corporation. The document, said to be leaked from Dublin Castle, disclosed a Government plan to carry out mass arrests, including senior Volunteers and other nationalists. In reality it was based on a response to a query on what precautions would be necessary in the event of enforcemnt of conscription, from the British GOC to the Chief Secretary in London. A sympathiser in the Castle had seen it and memorised the contents. The document that emerged may have been, to use recent parlance, 'sexed up'. In any case it persuaded Eoin MacNeill to issue a general order to the Volunteers to resist being disarmed.*

*The countdown to a rising had started. Far right: a request to Seán T O'Kelly by Patrick Pearse, on the 22nd, to put William and him up for the night – as "it is important that we should be in town". Near right: unflattering cartoon of Bulmer Hobson. A critic of the rising (it would be 'precipitate action'), he was detained by his IRB colleagues on Good Friday afternoon.*

THE BRITISH GOVERNMENT'S PLAN

. . . FOR . . .

SUPPRESSING THE IRISH VOLUNTEERS.

WHOLESALE ARRESTS AND MASSACRE DECIDED UPON.

ARCHBISHOP OF DUBLIN TO BE MADE PRISONER.

The following is a transcript of a secret document in cipher at present in Dublin Castle. It is made public by a High Official whose conscience revolted when he learned the details of the plot.

"The following measures have been sanctioned by the Irish Office on the recommendation of the General Officer Commanding the Forces in Ireland. All preparations will be made to put these measures in force immediately on receipt of an order issued from the Chief Secretary's Office, Dublin Castle, and signed by the Under Secretary and the General Officer Commanding the Forces in Ireland. First, the following persons to be placed under arrest:—All members of the Sinn Fein National Council; the Central Executive Irish Sinn Fein Volunteers; General Council Irish Sinn Fein Volunteers; County Board Irish Sinn Fein Volunteer's; Executive Committee National Volunteers; Coisde Gnota Committee Gaelic League. See List (a) three and four and Supplementary List (a) two . . . . . .

. . . . . . . Dublin Metropolitan Police and Royal Irish Constabulary Forces in Dublin City will be confined to barracks under direction of Competent Military Authority. An order will be issued to inhabitants of city to remain in their houses until such time as Competent Military Authority may otherwise direct or permit; pickets chosen from units of territorial force will be placed at all points marked on maps three and four accompanying; mounted patrols will continuously visit all points and report every hour. The following premises will be occupied by adequate forces and all necessary measures used without need of reference to headquarters:—First, premises known as Liberty Hall, Beresford Place; number six Harcourt Street, Sinn Fein Building; number two Dawson Street, Headquarters Volunteers; number twelve D'Olier Street, *Nationality* Office; number twenty-five Rutland Square, Gaelic League Office; number forty-one Rutland Square, Foresters' Hall; Sinn Fein Volunteer premises in city; all National Volunteer premises in city; Trade Council premises, Capel Street; Surrey House, Leinster Road, Rathmines. The following premises will be isolated and all communication to or from prevented: Premises known as Archbishop's House, Drumcondra; Mansion House, Dawson Street; number forty Herbert Park; Larkfield, Kimmage Road; Woodtown Park, Ballyboden; Saint Enda's College, Hermitage, Rathfarnham; and in addition premises in List five (d). See Maps three and four."

NOTE:—The reader will observe that this dastardly plan provides for the imprisonment of the spiritual, civic, and industrial guides of the people—the Archbishop, the Mansion House, and the Trades Council are to be prevented from interfering whilst the massacre of the Volunteers by the Military is in progress.



THE SUCCESSOR OF WOLFE TONE "BEG PARDON, CONSTABLE, BUT MAY WE HAVE A REVOLUTION"?
THE CONSTABLE: "CERTAINLY ME BHOY, AMUSE YERSELVES, BUT MIND, DONT BREAK ANY WINDOWS, ··· OR I'LL SUMMON YE."

Sgoil Éanna, Ráth Fearnáin. ST. ENDA'S COLLEGE, RATHFARNHAM.

95/2/1

22/4/16

A chara,

Could you put my brother and myself up to-night? It is important that we should be in town. If you cannot, can you get some friend to do it? Please let me know by bearer. We should send some traps in the early evening, and arrive on bicycles sometime later.

Mise

Pádraic Mac Piarais

Seán T. O'Ceallaigh
27 Upper Rutland St
Dublin

22 apl 1916

WOODTOWN PARK,
RATHFARNHAM,
CO. DUBLIN.

Volunteers completely deceived. All orders for special action are hereby cancelled, and on no account will action be taken.

Eoin MacNeill

Mc Donagh & I agree that it is important we have a conference immediately, as various messengers are awaiting decision.

Seumas

C.D. 94/4/1 (a)

*Eoin MacNeill (left) heard of the plans for the Rising on the night of Holy Thursday, 20th April. As news filtered through of the the failure of the 'Aud' arms expedition, at a meeting at a house in Rathgar (above), on the Saturday night he drafted an order (below, far left) that "Volunteers completely deceived. All orders for special action are hereby cancelled." The countermanding order was distributed by messengers to Volunteers around the country. MacNeill placed a cancellation notice to appear in the next day's 'Sunday Independent'.*

*Near left: message from James Connolly to Éamonn Ceannt (Commandant of the 4th Battalion) summoning him to a meeting of the Military Council in Liberty Hall to be held early on Easter Sunday morning. After much debate the leaders decided to carry on with the rising. It was deferred to noon on Easter Monday, to allow for the remobilisation of Volunteers.*

*Chapter 2*

# An Irish Republic is Proclaimed

Monday – Wednesday

*Despite the loss of the arms shipment and MacNeill's countermand, the IRB Military Council decided to proceed with the Rising on Easter Monday. Men and women assembled at Liberty Hall at midday and marched under Connolly to take over the GPO, where Pearse read the Proclamation of the Republic. Volunteer battalions and the ICA took over strategic locations at compass points around the city. The British military soon reacted: troops were rushed to Dublin Castle and reinforcements ordered to the city. At the GPO, after an early skirmish with Lancers, the first days were mostly quiet. The fight became intense in other locations. City Hall was taken by troops who charged from Dublin Castle. On Tuesday, British soldiers, ensconced in the Shelbourne Hotel, cleared the Green of the ICA, who then retreated to the College of Surgeons. There were clashes at the SDU and around the Four Courts. Seán Heuston fiercely defended the Mendicity Institution, which was taken by Wednesday. A detachment of Sherwood Foresters landed at Kingstown, attacked the lightly manned outposts near Mount Street Bridge and suffered heavy casualties. By Wednesday evening most of the republican forces were still in place, but British troops were flooding the city as they set about cordoning off much of Dublin.*

# POBLACHT NA H EIREANN.

## THE PROVISIONAL GOVERNMENT OF THE IRISH REPUBLIC

## TO THE PEOPLE OF IRELAND.

IRISHMEN AND IRISHWOMEN: In the name of God and of the dead generations from which she receives her old tradition of nationhood, Ireland, through us, summons her children to her flag and strikes for her freedom.

Having organised and trained her manhood through her secret revolutionary organisation, the Irish Republican Brotherhood, and through her open military organisations, the Irish Volunteers and the Irish Citizen Army, having patiently perfected her discipline, having resolutely waited for the right moment to reveal itself, she now seizes that moment, and, supported by her exiled children in America and by gallant allies in Europe, but relying in the first on her own strength, she strikes in full confidence of victory.

We declare the right of the people of Ireland to the ownership of Ireland, and to the unfettered control of Irish destinies, to be sovereign and indefeasible. The long usurpation of that right by a foreign people and government has not extinguished the right, nor can it ever be extinguished except by the destruction of the Irish people. In every generation the Irish people have asserted their right to national freedom and sovereignty; six times during the past three hundred years they have asserted it in arms. Standing on that fundamental right and again asserting it in arms in the face of the world, we hereby proclaim the Irish Republic as a Sovereign Independent State, and we pledge our lives and the lives of our comrades-in-arms to the cause of its freedom, of its welfare, and of its exaltation among the nations.

The Irish Republic is entitled to, and hereby claims, the allegiance of every Irishman and Irishwoman. The Republic guarantees religious and civil liberty, equal rights and equal opportunities to all its citizens, and declares its resolve to pursue the happiness and prosperity of the whole nation and of all its parts, cherishing all the children of the nation equally, and oblivious of the differences carefully fostered by an alien government, which have divided a minority from the majority in the past.

Until our arms have brought the opportune moment for the establishment of a permanent National Government, representative of the whole people of Ireland and elected by the suffrages of all her men and women, the Provisional Government, hereby constituted, will administer the civil and military affairs of the Republic in trust for the people.

We place the cause of the Irish Republic under the protection of the Most High God, Whose blessing we invoke upon our arms, and we pray that no one who serves that cause will dishonour it by cowardice, inhumanity, or rapine. In this supreme hour the Irish nation must, by its valour and discipline and by the readiness of its children to sacrifice themselves for the common good, prove itself worthyof the august destiny to which it is called.

Signed on Behalf of the Provisional Government,

THOMAS J. CLARKE,

SEAN Mac DIARMADA, THOMAS MacDONAGH,

P. H. PEARSE, EAMONN CEANNT,

JAMES CONNOLLY. JOSEPH PLUNKETT.

*Set in bronze: signatories of the Proclamation of the Irish Republic, (together with The O'Rahilly) above. The Proclamation (left) was clear and inspirational. God is invoked. It sets out the central role of the IRB, and (over-optimistically, as it turned out) refers to the support of the 'gallant allies in Europe'. Continuity with the centuries of revolutionary separatism is stated. Thought to be mainly written by Pearse, Connolly's hand can be seen in the assertion of the right of the Irish people to the ownership of Ireland. It was progressive: claiming the allegiance of Irishwomen as well as Irishmen. With an eye on the North, it offered religious as well as civil liberty – and decried the differences 'fostered by an alien government', which it said divided the minority from a majority.*

*On Easter Sunday night, 2,500 copies of the Proclamation were printed in a tiny room at Liberty Hall, on an old Wharfedale stop-cylinder similar to this one, right. Short of type, the printer and compositors had to print in two halves as well as resorting to other improvisations such as using sealing wax to convert a large P into an R, needed for 'IRISH' (fourth line).*

*Right: Company mobilisation order, signed by Patrick Pearse in his typical sloping backhand style.*

*On Easter Monday morning, all over Dublin, Volunteers and members of the Irish Citizen Army left their homes and families. Many felt that they would not survive the coming battle. Others felt exhilaration. Some were surprised, when they assembled – they had not harboured any idea that a rising was upon them.*

*Near right: Larkfield Mill, Kimmage. On Monday, around 60 Volunteers (mainly from Britain) set out from here on a tram to the city centre. In a surprisingly law-abiding start to a rising, George Plunkett paid the fare for all.*

*The countermanding order led to the need for rapid coordination on the Monday; note from Cathal Brugha to Commandant Éamonn Ceannt, at the 4th Battalion assembly area, far right.*

IRISH VOLUNTEERS.
DUBLIN BRIGADE.

COMPANY MOBILISATION ORDER.

The E Coy., 4th Batt., will mobilise ~~to-day~~ Easter Sunday at the hour of 2.45 p.m.

Point of Mobilisation Rathfarnham Chapel

Full Service Equipment to be worn, including overcoat, haversack, water-bottle, canteen, full arms & ammunition.

Rations for eight hours to be carried.

Cycle Scouts to be mounted, and ALL men having cycles or motor cycles to bring them.

P. H. Pearse
Captain or Officer Commanding.

Dated this 20th day of April, 1916.

To Comdt. Kent
Emerald Square

Only 4 more has turned up in addition to the messenger. What time shall I leave? Hope you got my message re not being able to procure tape.

Cathal Brugha

10.22 Am
24.4.16
per Cyclist

41

*Above: statue of James Connolly, on Beresford Place, facing the present-day Liberty Hall.*

*Left: Liberty Hall, with the ICA making clear their attitude to WW I. A mixed force of ICA and Irish Volunteers assembled here on Easter Monday morning, 24th April and lined up before James Connolly. Just before noon the main formation, (designated the Headquarters Battalion) headed for the GPO, followed by carts carrying ammunition, weapons and other supplies. Detachments also set off for St Stephen's Green (under Michael Mallin) and the Mendicity Institution (under Seán Heuston).*

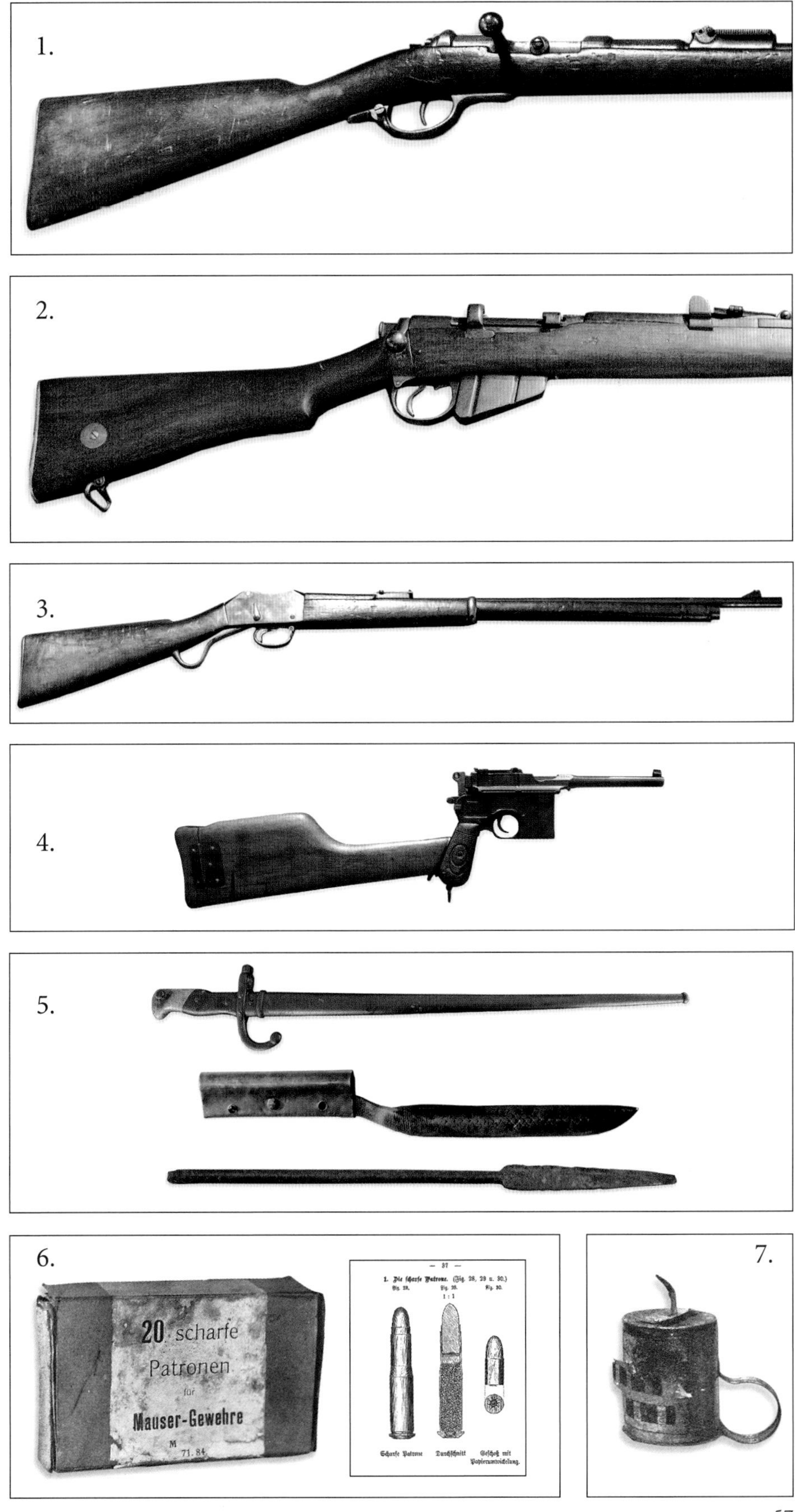


*The republican forces fielded an eclectic range of weapons: (not to scale)*

*1. (Howth) Mauser 71. These were bolt-action rifles issued to the Prussian Army in 1872, revolutionary for their time. Big, heavy rifles, they were still in good condition in 1916. Their Achilles heel was that they were single shot.*

*2. The service British Lee Enfield SMLE, with its ten-round magazine. Volunteers had purloined some from soldiers. It could be fired at around 15 rounds per minute as opposed to four for the Mauser 71.*

*3. The single-shot Martini-Henry, known as a weapon of empire. It had been standard issue to the RIC.*

*4. Mauser 'Broomhandle' C96, this semi-automatic pistol with a detachable stock proved effective at Mount Street. It was also used by Markievicz at St Stephen's Green and Brugha at the SDU.*

*5. French sword-type bayonet in scabbard; improvised bayonet for shotgun; primitive pike-head – some pikes were prepared for use, giving resonances of the 1798 rebellion.*

*6. Packet of 20 Mauser cartridges and extract from the manual showing diagrams of the 11 mm black powder cartridges with a lead bullet.*

*7. Improvised bomb; cans filled with explosive, with a projecting fuse.*

*Left: Trams terminate at the General Post Office and Nelson's Pillar – a busy scene on Sackville Street as it was before the Rising. The Post Office then played an important role in Irish life; the GPO was the communications hub and a focal point of Sackville Street. 'Large and sober' (as described by architectural historian Christine Casey), it was purpose-built as the main post office to a design by Francis Johnston and completed in 1818.*

*Below left: the GPO. On Easter Monday, just after midday, James Connolly led his column of Volunteers and ICA to halt outside the portico, ordered "left turn", then "charge". They swarmed through the main doorway and spread out.*

*Below: 'leaders of the insurrection', most of whom were executed within a week of the Rising's end.*

*Above: the public area today. After the Rising, the only part of the GPO more or less intact was the facade. The rest of the building was completely reconstructed during the years 1924-29.*

*Right: the GPO public office, on the eve of the Rising. Francis Johnston's building had just been extensively re-modelled and had re-opened a month before the Rising. The public telephone box in the middle was used to imprison a captured British lieutenant .*

*Left: the portico of the GPO. Soon after the takeover of the building, Commandant-General Pearse stepped out here and read the Proclamation of the Irish Republic to a small bemused crowd of bystanders. Then Connolly shook his hand and said: "Thanks be to God, Pearse, that we have lived to see this day!"*

*At around 1:15 pm on Easter Monday there was the first encounter with the British Army, a bloody one. A detachment of Lancers, from Marlborough (now McKee) Barracks, had been assigned to investigate reports of insurgency in the city centre. Pausing briefly at the Parnell Monument, they rode south along Sackville Street in perfect order, at a gallop, lances at the ready. Connolly had given orders that those within the GPO were to hold fire until the party of soldiers had galloped the full length of the GPO. However, as the first of the Lancers passed Nelson's Pillar, some Volunteers opened fire with a scattered volley. Four soldiers toppled over; three were dead (depiction, left). The colonel in charge ordered them to pull back and they retreated, leaving behind both men and horses. Interestingly, General Maxwell did not include this inglorious defeat in his official account of the week's activities.*

*Near right: On Monday evening Seán MacDermott sent this scribbled note from 'Headquarters, Irish Republican Government' to the IRB captors of Bulmer Hobson, in captivity at Phibsborough, to release him as "everything splendid" – there was no worry now of Hobson being able to impede the Rising.*

*Far right: Sackville Street as seen from O'Connell Bridge. Commandant-General Connolly ordered men to occupy buildings on both sides of the street, especially those at the southern end that dominated the approaches at the bridge: Kelly's shooting and tackle premises on the left, and Hopkins and Hopkins' jewellers on the right.*

*Right: the 'Irish War News' was issued on Tuesday. The article on the front cover had been pre-prepared for another nationalist periodical but used here.* *(See page 199 for the text of this thought-provoking piece.)* *The bulletin included as a STOP PRESS on the back page Pearse's communiqué that the Irish Republic had been proclaimed. A run of 12,000 copies was printed in a commandeered print works at Halston Street. Connolly and Pearse later decided that they would abandon the idea of a second issue, but issue a handbill-style proclamation instead.*

# IRISH WAR NEWS

## THE IRISH REPUBLIC.

Vol. 1. No. 1 — DUBLIN, TUESDAY, APRIL 25, 1916. — One Penny

### "IF THE GERMANS CONQUERED ENGLAND."

In the London "New Statesman" for *April 1st*, an article is published—"If the Germans Conquered England," which has the appearance of a very clever piece of satire written by an Irishman. The writer draws a picture of England under German rule, almost every detail of which exactly fits the case of Ireland at the present day. Some of the sentences are so exquisitely appropriate that it is impossible to believe that the writer had not Ireland in his mind when he wrote them. For instance :—

"England would be constantly irritated by the lofty moral utterances of German statesmen who would assert—quite sincerely, no doubt—that England was free, freer indeed than she had ever been before. Prussian freedom, they would explain, was the only real freedom, and therefore England was free. They would point to the flourishing railways and farms and colleges. They would possibly point to the contingent of M.P's, which was permitted, in spite of its deplorable disorderliness, to sit in a permanent minority in the Reichstag. And not only would the Englishman have to listen to a constant flow of speeches of this sort ; he would find a respectable official Press secret bought over by the Government to say the same kind of things over and over, every day of the week. He would find, too, that his children were coming home from school with new ideas of history. . . . They would ask him if it was true that until the Germans came England had been an unruly country, constantly engaged in civil war. . . . The object of every schoolbook would be to make the English child grow up in the notion that the history of his country was a thing to forget, and that the one bright spot in it was the fact that it had been conquered by cultured Germany."

"If there was a revolt, German statesmen would deliver grave speeches about "disloyalty," "ingratitude," "reckless agitators who would ruin their country's prosperity. . . . Prussian soldiers would be encamped in every barracks—the English conscripts having been sent out of the country to be trained in Germany, or to fight the Chinese—in order to come to the aid of German morality, should English sedition come to blows with it."

"England would be exhorted to abandon her own genius in order to imitate the genius of her conquerors, to forget her own history for a larger history, to give up her own language for a "universal" language—in other words, to destroy her household gods one by one, and put in their place

1
2
3
4
5
6
7
8
9

*From Monday afternoon looting began in Sackville Street and its vicinity. Dublin's poor, sensing the absence of the law, seized the moment and carted away an array of loot. The Volunteers lacked numbers to prevent the looting.*

*Right: Charles Saurin depicts Pearse in the GPO telling Volunteers from Fairview, on Tuesday evening, that Dublin had now regained its honour, lost by not supporting Emmet's 1803 rising.*

*Volunteers reactivated a transmitter at the Irish School of Wireless, right, on Sackville and Lower Abbey Street, above Reis's premises. After some difficulty they broadcast in Morse code the news of the Rising. At 1:35 pm on Tuesday a naval ship at Kingstown intercepted the message 'Irish Republic declared in Dublin today... Irish troops have captured city...'*

*On Tuesday night Connolly ordered the occupation of the nearby Hotel Metropole: poster, near right. Far right: pass signed by him on hotel paper.*

*Left: schematic drawing of the GPO as it was early in the week: 1 public office; 2 arms store; 3 sick bay; 4 entrance door; 5 barricaded windows; 6 office; 7 message arrangement to other side of street (made of twine and a can); 8 snipers on roof; 9 van yard.*

Hotel Metropole

(SACKVILLE STREET).

DUBLIN, 25th April 1916.

Please pass Mr. ............... who is leaving Dublin for Leeds.

and oblige,

Manager.

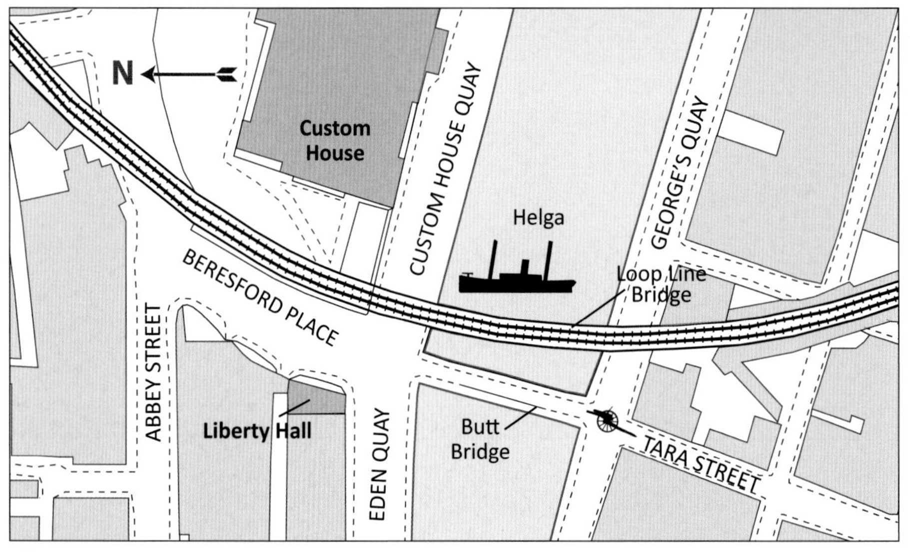


*The Germans had previously agreed that there would be a naval demonstration, in tandem with the landing from the 'Aud', and the Rising in Dublin. And it was quite a demontration, albeit against an undefended coastal town. At 4:10 am on 25th April four battle cruisers, with six light cruisers supported by destroyers, opened fire on Lowestoft on the North Sea coast. The action lasted ten minutes, after which the squadron went on to briefly shell Yarmouth. In all, 200 houses were damaged and four people were killed. Above left: a policeman searches through the rubble of a convalescent home which was destroyed.*

*Bombardment on a more modest scale: at 8 am on Wednesday, 'HMY Helga' dropped anchor by the Loop Line Bridge in front of the Custom House, where, according to an account, a Guinness ship was moored. The 'Helga', a fishery protection vessel, built in Dublin in 1908, was used as an anti-submarine patrol vessel after the war broke out. Using its QF 12-pounder, it opened fire on Liberty Hall, now abandoned, except for a caretaker. Its log records 24 rounds being fired.*

*Left: map of the Liberty Hall area.*

*Right: the Loop Line Bridge. The gun had to fire under the bridge towards Liberty Hall. It initially hit the bridge by one account; another suggests that it tried to reach the hall by firing parabolically (an 'up' and 'over' shot) from further down the river. That morning, Trinity OTC members, in civilian attire, had tried to hack holes into the road surface at Tara Street, to provide an anchor against artillery recoil. The British wheeled two 18-pounders from Trinity, set up on Tara Street and shelled Liberty Hall. Right: 18-pounder shells, coming from the Tara Street direction (rather than the frontal shells from the 'Helga') caused the principal damage, seen on the left hand side; the adjacent building on the right suffered heavily. Guns in high places: the British placed machine guns at various high points to pour fire on rebel positions. These included the roof of the Custom House and, below near right, Tara Street Fire Station. Soldiers on the buildings overlooking O'Connell Bridge and at McBirney's store (middle and far right) were able to cover republican positions on Lower Sackville Street. Overleaf: the Liffey, Loop Line Bridge and Custom House as seen from the new Liberty Hall of 1965.*

BUS

Ulster Bank Group
NO ENTRY

*On Easter Monday an ICA column under Captain Seán Connolly headed from Liberty Hall towards Dublin Castle.*
*An unarmed Constable, James O'Brien of the Dublin Metropolitan Police (DMP), attempted to stop the ICA unit at his post (left, circled) by the upper Castle gate at Cork Hill. As O'Brien put out his arm, Seán Connolly raised his rifle and shot him. Coincidentally, a meeting had just started some 25 metres away. Sir Matthew Nathan, Under-Secretary for Ireland, Major Ivor Price, Chief Military Intelligence officer and Arthur Hamilton Norway, head of the Post Office, demonstrating how important the postal communications role was in security matters, were planning the arrest of the leaders of the 'Sinn Féiners'. Major Price ran out into the upper Castle yard and fired his revolver. He withdrew then to organise the Castle defences. The British response was soon in coming.*

*Left: in uniform, the unfortunate Constable James O'Brien (illustrating that the DMP were generally men of an impressive height.) The DMP was an unarmed force. They were withdrawn after the beginning of the Rising, and took no direct part in the fighting.*

*Right: the Cork Hill entrance to Dublin Castle, the bastion of English rule since the Anglo-Norman invasion. It was still the centre of British administration and security control of Ireland. Set back a little from the main thoroughfares of early 20th-century Dublin, it may not have been the decisive strategic point that many historians have claimed was worth capturing. However, its seizure would have been worthwhile in symbolic terms, not to mention that it had been the objective of Robert Emmet's failed 1803 rebellion (a constant inspiration for Pearse).*

*Right: looking from the arcade outside the Castle guardroom towards Cork Hill and City Hall. An assault party charged the guardroom and threw a cannister bomb which failed to explode. They overpowered the six startled soldiers within. The ICA did not proceed into the Castle. A military historian has written that it was obvious their orders were not to attack the Castle as "no military leader would entrust this...to a force of ten men." Demonstrating the need for good advance intelligence in any conflict, the insurgents did not know that the Castle was lightly guarded, with only around 25 soldiers in Ship Street Barracks at the rear.*

*Seán Connolly ordered the occupation of the 'Mail' and 'Express' offices, far left, on Cork Hill, and the premises of Henry and James, Tailors, on the corner of Parliament Street. He also assigned men to the Dublin Corporation rates office (formerly the Newcomen Bank). Near left: commemorative plaque at City Hall.*

*The British soon recovered. The Dublin Garrison adjutant received a message from the DMP at 12:15 pm that the Castle was being attacked by 'armed Sinn Feiners'. He ordered all available troops from Portobello, Richmond and Royal barracks to proceed to Dublin Castle. By 2 pm 180 troops had reached the Ship Street entrance. The troops fanned out and set up on roofs and towers within the Castle complex, from where they began to pour fire on the ICA positions.*

*Left: sketch of John Connolly (no relation of James Connolly), known as Seán. An actor in the Abbey company, he was 33 years of age. Ironically, in light of Emmet's aspiration to seize Dublin Castle, Connolly had acted in a play by Lennox Robinson on Emmet's failed rebellion. He had only recently appeared in James Connolly's play 'Under Which Flag' at Liberty Hall.*

Above: *chimneys and dome – the complex and cluttered roof of City Hall, surrounded by balustrades. Seán Connolly was by the dome when he was shot by a British sniper at around 2 pm on Monday. Dr Kathleen Lynn, a captain and medical officer of the ICA, attended him as as he lay dying.*

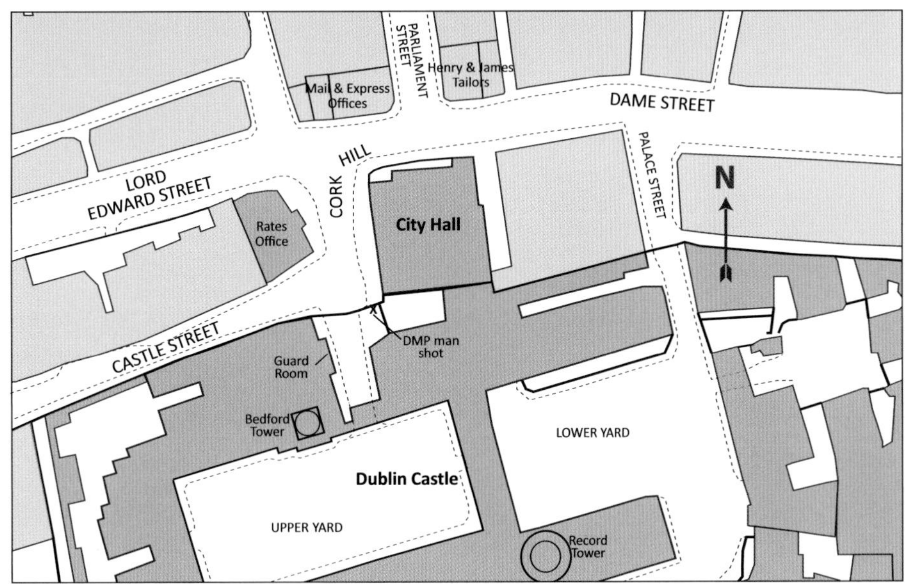


*Right: map of the Dublin Castle area.*

*Left: the upper gate to the Castle, at Cork Hill, seen from the City Hall roof.*

*Originally bare of defenders, the Castle was now swarming with troops. Supported by heavy machine-gun fire (Dr Lynn later wrote that "the bullets fell like rain"), the British launched a fierce assault on City Hall on Monday evening. They were repelled by fire from the roof of the 'Mail' and 'Express' building, as well as from the Henry and James premises.*

*Persistent, the British troops attacked in surges. They forced their way into the ground floor of City Hall, through a back window. Surrounded, Kathleen Lynn and her comrades surrendered. The party on the roof held out until dawn on Tuesday.*

*Later on Tuesday, at around 2 pm, waves of troops emerged through the upper gate to attack the remaining rebel positions. Fire was also poured from the roof of City Hall, now in British hands. The troops broke through the front doors and stormed the stairs. Just before 3 pm, it ended: the survivors of the ICA garrison had climbed out the rear windows and slipped away.*

*Left: possible bullet holes at the portico of the rates office, at Cork Hill, opposite City Hall.*

*Above: the red-brick 'forts' viewed from City Hall roof – the former 'Mail' and 'Express' offices on the left of the intersection with Parliament Street; Henry and James on the right.*

*Near right: Kathleen Lynn. In 1919 this courageous woman founded a hospital for infants, St Ultan's, which recognised the poor socio-medical conditions in Dublin and focussed on children's health.*

*Far right: there are many bullet holes around the Rotunda of City Hall; this one is between the legs of the statue of Charles Lucas, an 18th-century physician.*

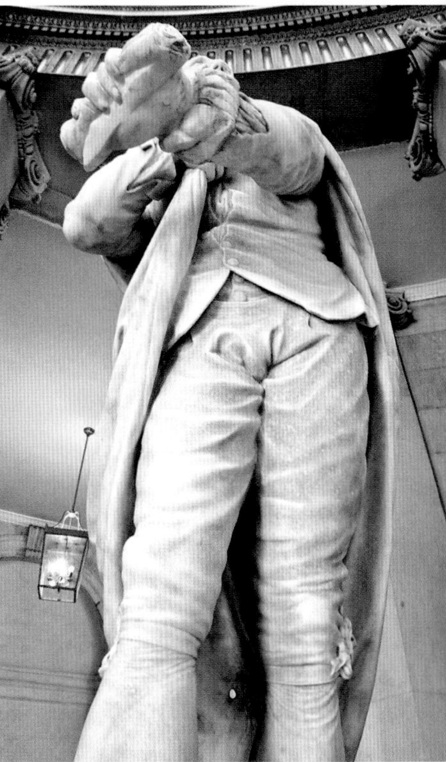

*The Volunteers had seized the telegraph exchange in the GPO. Some GPO personnel made their way to the Post Office telegraph office at Amiens Street Station and established contact with the Post Office in London via a cross-channel cable that ran through the station. The insurgents did not, however, seize the Crown Alley central telegraph exchange, left. It had been planned to destroy an adjacent cable manhole, but the Volunteers detailed for this did not show up. The exchange was occupied by troops on Monday evening. The British military response was rapid. At 12:30 pm on Monday the GOC Curragh Camp was telephoned and requested to send a mobile column by train to Kingsbridge. At 1:10 pm a message telling of the Rising was sent to the Navy at Kingstown and transmitted by wireless to London. By 2 pm Dublin Castle had been reinforced. By just after 5 pm, 1,600 men had arrived by train from the Curragh. Orders were sent for artillery from Athlone; Dublin Fusiliers from Templemore; more men from the Curragh as well as a composite battalion from Belfast. Later that day the 59th Division in England was mobilised.*

*Left: an inner cordon was established by midday on Tuesday.*

*Right: Brigadier-General W. Lowe, 3rd Reserve Cavalry Brigade, the Curragh, was given command of the British forces in the Dublin area. He detrained at Kingsbridge station early on Tuesday morning. By now around 4,600 British troops had been assembled in the city.*

*Lowe adopted a decisive and clear strategy to put down the rebellion. He ordered that a series of cordons be established. Firstly, an inner cordon made up of six posts was to run between Kingsbridge and Trinity College. It was completed by noon on Tuesday, with few losses. It cut the republican forces in two and allowed a line of communications and reinforcement.*

*Right: map from a post-Rising booklet. It shows the cordons set up by Lowe: heavy red line – inner cordon; lighter red – outer cordons; republican positions are circled in red.*

*As troops arrived, outer cordons were set up. A northern one was established from Kingsbridge along the North Circular Road to Amiens Street. A southern one was formed along the Grand Canal in a westerly direction to Kilmainham and Kingsbridge. By Tuesday evening Lowe had decided to ignore the SDU, Jacobs, and St Stephen's Green positions and concentrate on the GPO and the Four Courts.*

*All the tools necessary to suppress a rising: the principal weapons of the British Army in Dublin during 1916. (not to scale)*

*1. Short Magazine Lee Enfield Mk III. Firing a .303 bullet, with a 10-shot magazine, this was the general-issue service rifle during WW I. During the 1916 Rising, British troops could achieve a much higher rate of fire with this rifle than the opposing single-shot Howth Mausers.*

*2. Lewis machine gun, with ammunition pan. This relatively light machine gun (air-cooled using an aluminium barrel radiator) fired .303 bullets at 550 rounds per minute.*

*3. Webley, .455 calibre, six-shot, service revolver.*

*4. Vickers machine gun. This was the regular heavy machine gun of the British during WW I and for many decades afterwards. Solid and reliable, it was water-cooled and fed by a 250-round (.303 calibre) canvas belt.*

*5. 18-pounder field gun, standard British field artillery gun on the western front. Four of these were transported by train from the Reserve Artillery Brigade at Athlone to Dublin on Tuesday 25th April.*

*6. 18-pounder shell. Only shrapnel versions (anti-personnel, which emitted small balls) were available during the Rising.*

*Right: unlikely to approve of insurrection, Edmund Burke, philospher and statesman, guards Trinity College (which he entered in 1744). His book 'Reflections on the Revolution in France' (1790) argued that the revolution there would end disastrously.*

*The insurgents did not plan to occupy Trinity. In any case, they were too thinly stretched to garrison such a vast space. On Monday soon after midday, the Chief Steward gave the order to lock the Front Gate. A handful of the Dublin University Officer Training Corps (OTC) mustered. Captain Alton, right, took charge by 3 pm. The HQ of the OTC was at the Westland Row end and they kept a wary eye on the republicans patrolling the viaduct near Westland Row Railway Station. More OTC arrived as well as regular soldiers who were on leave. On Tuesday morning, firing parties were placed on the roofs. By evening a detachment of the Leinster Regiment had arrived. Machine guns were posted on commanding positions on the College buildings. The College had become a veritable and strategic fortress. An OTC officer later noted that it separated the "two important rebel storm centres, the GPO to the north and St Stephen's Green to the south".*

CAPT. E. H. ALTON,
OFFICER COMMANDING INFANTRY.

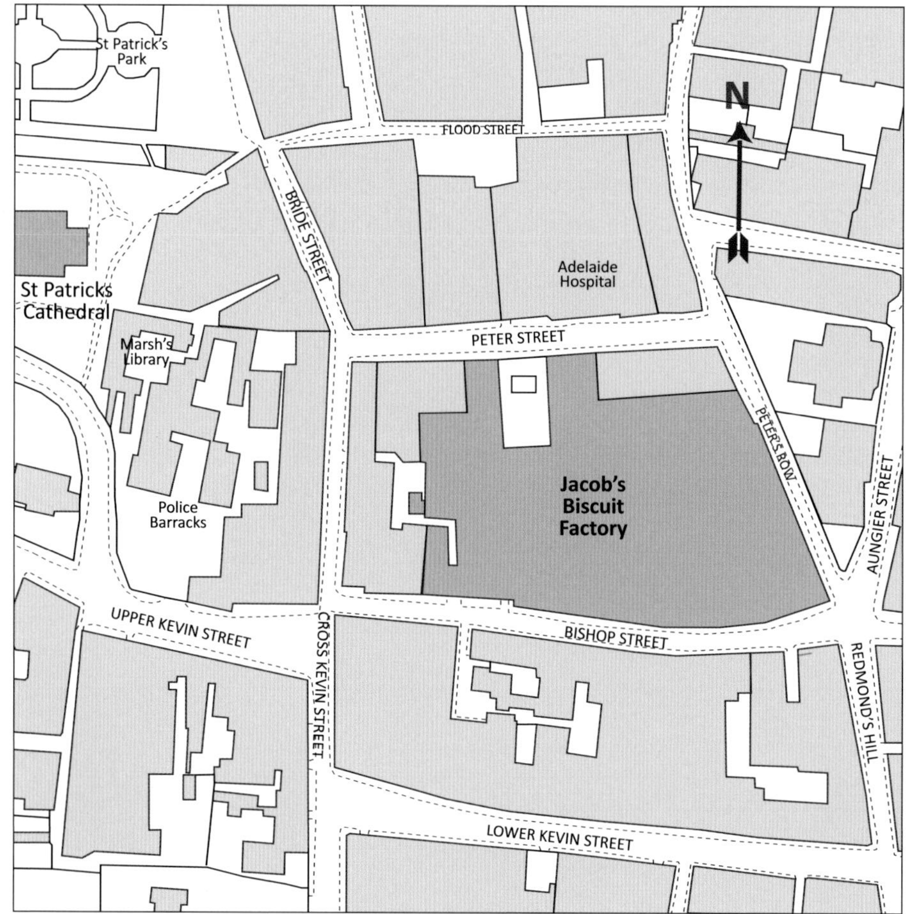


*Just before midday on Monday Commandant Thomas MacDonagh assembled his 2nd Battalion at St Stephen's Green and marched with around 150 men to occupy the Jacob's biscuit factory complex, at Bishop Street, above. Men were placed on roofs and towers. By Tuesday evening the British had decided to ignore Jacob's and concentrate on the GPO.*
*Left: map*
*Below: Bishop Street today.*

St Stephen's Green. As it is today (above); as it was pre-1916, right.

*A unit of the ICA under Commandant Michael Mallin arrived at St Stephen's Green and occupied the park. A first-aid post was established in a bandstand. They commenced to dig shallow defensive trenches covering the main entrances. Barricades were erected on the roads around the park. Countess Markievicz arrived and Mallin assigned her to his garrison. The Royal College of Surgeons (RCSI) was occupied on Monday afternoon.*

*Right: map of the area*

*Below: a trench in St Stephen's Green, as portrayed in the 'Daily Sketch'.*

Left: *the Victorian pile of the Shelbourne Hotel, on St Stephen's Green North. This had been renovated in 1865 under the direction of John McCurdy (who had just designed an extension to Kilmainham Gaol). On Easter Monday the hotel was packed with guests, who gazed at the strange events unfolding outside. The original plan was to take over this dominant structure, but Mallin was short of men. As it turned out, it would have been better to assign forces here than to have them dig trenches in the park.*

*Left: a view from on high at the Shelbourne, a century ago.*

*Below left: sketch of a barricade outside the Shelbourne. Usually barricades were to block movement (although there was a fierce engagement from the 1st Battalion barricades by Church Street). They were made up of commandeered materials, including furniture, horse drays, motor vehicles, and – in Sackville Street – a tram.*

*Below: bust of Countess Markievicz, appropriately in St Stephen's Green.*

*Above: a present-day view of St Stephen's Green from the commanding heights of the Shelbourne.*

*A British officer reconnoitered the area late on Monday. Recognising the strategic importance of the Shelbourne, it was decided to occupy it. After midnight, troops left Dublin Castle and entered the hotel. They also took over the United Services Club, right, at the western end of the street, where they placed a Lewis gun. In the hotel, snipers were deployed and a Vickers machine gun was installed at a window on the fourth floor. At 4 am the British opened fire from both the hotel and the club. A hail of bullets cut through the trees and lashed the ICA in the Green. Over the next hours, they fell back to the RCSI with heavy losses.*

*Above: a present-day fish-eye view from the roof of the RCSI.*
*Left: the RCSI (by Edward Parke, 1805) at the western side of the Green.*
*The ICA spread out in the College and barricaded windows. Riflemen on the roof exchanged fire with the British in the Shelbourne Hotel and the United Services Club, from where the Lewis gun probably created some of these bullet holes on the Fusiliers' Arch (below) at the north-west entrance to the park.*

*On Monday a section of the ICA had been assigned to hold southern positions temporarily and so allow the main force to set up in the St Stephen's Green area. To interdict possible troop trains, they took over Harcourt Street Station (near right, today, formerly the Dublin & Wicklow Railway terminus). ICA men spread out along the elevated railway line (including over this bridge, far right, by Harcourt Road, seen in the 1950s before its removal). An intention was to provide flanking support from the railway bridge over the canal to a ICA unit assigned to Davy's public house, to the west.*

*Above: a present-day view of Portobello Harbour.*

*Just after midday on Monday, an ICA unit reached Davy's public house, left, located by Portobello bridge and harbour over the Grand Canal. The intention was to protect the positions in the Green by intercepting troops from Portobello Barracks. One of the rebels, one James Joyce (no relation) happened to be an employee. As Davy, the proprietor, proceeded to sack Joyce, he was summarily ejected.*

*Portobello (now Cathal Brugha) Barracks parade ground, right, had an available complement of 600 men of the 3rd Battalion, Royal Irish Rifles. On receiving the news of the assault on Dublin Castle, 50 soldiers were sent to strengthen the position.*

*As the soldiers approached Portobello Bridge a fusilade of shots burst out from Davy's. Reinforcements arrived and a Maxim machine gun (on wheels, the predecessor of the Vickers) was positioned at the bridge. With riflemen lining the southern banks the British poured heavy fire on the public house. The ICA slipped away out the back and withdrew to the positions at St Stephen's Green.*

*The British troops, still trundling the Maxim, were now able to continue along Camden Street. Men of the 2nd Battalion (from the garrison occupying Jacob's factory) had been posted in various outsposts along the street. They opened fire on an advance party of the troops, who retreated. The main party took an alternative route and safely reached Dublin Castle at around 2 pm.*

*Right: Portobello (La Touche) Bridge over the Grand Canal. The public house (formerly Davy's) is on the right.*

Captain J. C. Bowen=Colthurst.

*On Monday, Francis Sheehy-Skeffington, (far left, on the right) a quixotic pacifist, had braved gunfire to help a British officer wounded at Dublin Castle. Later, in Sackville Street, he had unsuccessfully appealed to looters to disperse. On Tuesday, he put up posters in central Dublin calling for a meeting of citizens to band together against looting. On his way home for supper before the meeting, he approached Portobello Bridge, at around 6 pm, followed by a crowd. A lieutenant on picket duty at Davy's pub ordered him to be arrested and brought to Portobello Barracks. All there were jittery – firing could be heard from the rebel position at Jacob's factory and they were expecting an imminent attack.*

*No one was more agitated than Captain John Bowen-Colthurst, (above, near right). A veteran of the Boer War, from a landed family in Co. Cork, he was in the barracks as a result of what was deemed 'shell shock' from fighting in France. Between 10 and 11 pm, he charged into the guardroom and demanded that Sheehy-Skeffington be handed over. He set off with a raiding party from the barracks, down Military Road, left. Sheehy-Skeffington was bound with a cord.*

*Reaching the intersection with Rathmines Road, Bowen-Colthurst intercepted three youths. One, 17-year-old James Coade (near right) had earlier been at a sodality meeting at the nearby Catholic church. He was now returning home. Bowen-Colthurst shouted at them that martial law had been proclaimed and that he could shoot them. Bowen-Colthurst gave the order: "bash him" – Coade was hit by a rifle butt in the jaw. As Coade went away Bowen-Colthurst drew his revolver and shot him in the back through the abdomen. The youth died of his wound the next morning.*

*The raiding party continued towards Portobello Bridge, where Sheehy-Skeffington was left under guard, Bowen-Colthurst ordering that the unfortunate pacifist be shot if they were fired on. About three hundred metres on, the party raided Alderman James Kelly's tobacco shop at Kelly's corner (above, far right), having mistaken him for another alderman, a 'Sinn Féiner', of the same surname. The troops fired at the shop and threw a grenade. They seized four men, who had sought refuge in the basement, and brought them back to the barracks.*

*Right: map of the Rathmines and Portobello area.*

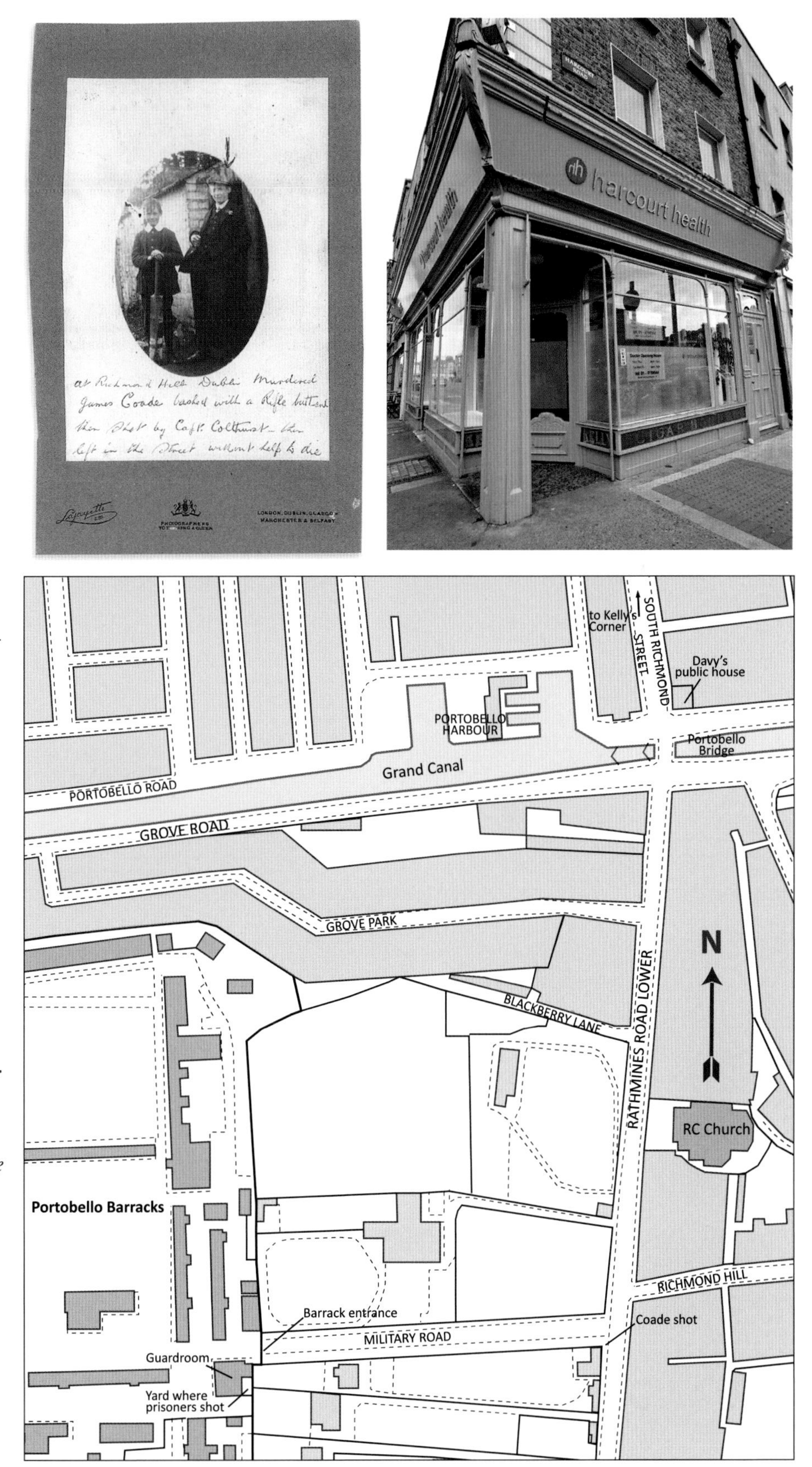

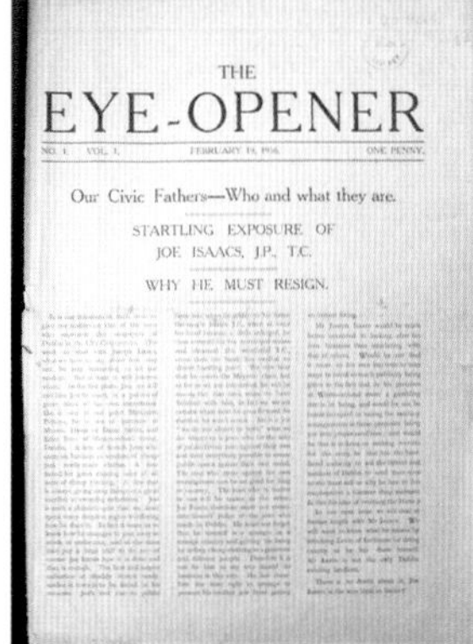

THE
EYE-OPENER

ONE PENNY.

Our Civic Fathers—Who and what they are.

STARTLING EXPOSURE OF
JOE ISAACS, J.P., T.C.

WHY HE MUST RESIGN.

*Above: 'The Eye-Opener' periodical, a miscellany of muted titillation and manufactured outrage.*

*Two of the men seized at Kelly's premises were journalists, editors of minor periodicals, innocent and innocuous. One was Patrick MacIntyre, anti-Larkinite editor of 'The Searchlight'. The other was Thomas Dickson, left, originally from Glasgow, editor of 'The Eye-Opener'. Dickson told his fellow captives that he intended to issue a loyalist special edition. Even in the guardroom there was a class pecking-order and Sheehy Skeffington was housed in one of the individual cells like this one, left. The other two had to share with other prisoners.*

*Bowen-Colthurst sat up late into the night, praying. Eventually he lighted on a suitably bloodthirsty biblical text from St Luke: "And these mine enemies, which will not have me to rule over them, bring them forth and slay them."*

*At 10:20 am Bowen-Colthurst arrived in the guardroom and said he wanted Sheehy-Skeffington, Dickson and MacIntyre in the yard. He said he was going to shoot them as it seemed "the best thing to be done". The prisoners were ordered to the wall (cross, right). Bowen-Colthurst summoned seven soldiers and ordered them to fire at the prisoners, who were neither blindfolded, nor bound. Sheehy Skeffington was shot again after movement was seen. Bowen-Colthurst reported what he had done to the barrack commander, who ordered that he not leave the precincts. The bodies were buried in the barracks, the yard was scrubbed and the bricks with bullet holes were replaced. Bowen-Colthurst raided Sheehy-Skeffington's house on the Friday to seek incriminating documents.*

*Major Sir Francis Vane had been setting up an observation post at Rathmines Town Hall, near right, when he heard of the murders. He was appalled at the inaction of the army and travelled to see Lord Kitchener in London. Eventually a court martial was held. Bowen-Colthurst was found guilty of murder but (conveniently) deemed insane – he was then sent to Broadmoor.*

*Far right: memorial outside the barracks gate.*

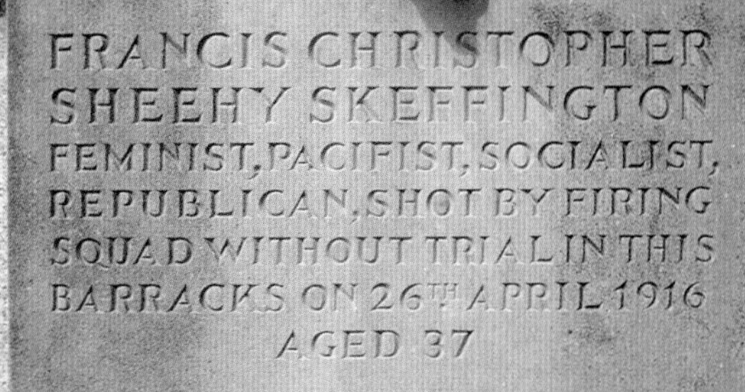

*Above: the Magazine Fort, Phoenix Park, dating from 1738, where army ordnance was stored. The fort is around 60 metres square, with four demi-bastions and a moat.*

*Just after midday on Monday, around 30 men, led by Paddy Daly (later to gain notoriety as a pro-Treaty general in Civil War Kerry) arrived here. Using the ruse of playing football, they disarmed the guards and rushed in (entrance, left). Unable to access the main magazine, they set their explosive charges against its wall. As well as soldiers, prisoners included the wife and family of the fort's commander (who was abroad).*

*The prisoners were allowed leave but told not to raise the alarm. Gathering a quantity of arms and ammunition, the Volunteers headed back to their battallion at Church Street. As they left, they saw George Playfair (23), son of the fort's commander, dashing away. Volunteer Garry Holohan followed him on a bicycle. Playfair ran out the Islandbridge Gate, right, and spoke to a policeman.*

*Below: as it was – Islandbridge Gate and Lodge.*

*Playfair ran to nearby Park Place, where there were military residences. He frantically knocked on the door of this house, above. As the door was being opened, Garry Holohan came up, shot him and Playfair fell, mortally wounded.*
*Left: George Playfair's grave, Hibernian Military School, Phoenix Park.*
*Below: telegram requesting Playfair's father's presence.*

A.
POST OFFICE TELEGRAPHS.
(Inland Telegrams.)
For Postage Stamps.

TO Gunshot London

Eldest son of Captain Playfair ordnance Hovre dangerously wounded yesterday aaa if possible can father come to Dublin

FROM Guncotton Dublin

The Name and Address of the Sender, IF NOT TO BE TELEGRAPHED, must be written in the Space provided at the Back of the Form.

10.10am

*Right: granite fortress – Gandon's Four Courts.*

*The 1st Battalion assembled at a hall at Blackhall Street at 11 am on Monday: objective – to occupy a line from Cabra to the quays. Commandant Edward Daly assigned his men: one company to occupy the Four Courts (a primary objective); another to Brunswick and Upper Church Streets. Another was to take over Broadstone Station but this unit decided that they had not enough men and occupied tenement houses in North King Street instead. Barricades were set up in and around Church Street. Just after midday, 50 Lancers of the 6th Reserve Cavalry Regiment were escorting LNWR lorries carrying rifles and grenades from North Wall (right, Lancers on the quays, after the Rising). As they passed the intersection with Church Street they came under fire. The lead Lancer was killed and the rest took shelter nearby. A fallen lance was taken and, supporting a tricolour, propped at the intersection of North King and Church Streets, where it remained for the rest of the week.*

*Right: the junction of Charles Street (where the Lancers sheltered) and Ormond Quay, with the eastern end of the Four Courts in the background.*

Place
e Boys at the
Barracades

Pass Bearer
Mrs Heron
everywhere

From E Daly

*Near left: the youngest of the commandants, Edward Daly.*
*Far left: in light green, the sprawling territory assigned to Daly's 1st Battalion.*
*Right: intersection of present-day Church Street (a much narrower street in 1916) with the quays, where a barricade was placed on Monday by Whitworth Bridge.*
*Right: the former Richmond hospital on North Brunswick Street. It later catered for about 25 wounded rebels. Daly initially established his headquarters at St John's Convent, next door, where he was given a warm welcome by the Sisters of Charity. A field medical hospital was set up at the Fr Mathew Hall on Church Street.*
*Far left: looking south from the Constitution Hill direction, the multi-storey Clarke's Dairy at a narrow point along Church Street. This bottleneck commanded the approaches from Broadstone. The Volunteers occupied this and several other nearby buildings.*
*Near left: to 'the Boys at the Barricades' – pass issued by Daly.*
*When the Volunteers searched the Bridewell, right, they found 23 members of the DMP, as well as two Lancers, hiding in the cells, who were subsequently held prisoner in the Four Courts.*

Soon after midnight on Monday, military transport wagons headed east along the south quays. Fire came from the barricades by Whitworth Bridge and the British withdrew.

In a move that was to have serious implications for the Rising, four 18-pounder field guns sent by train from Athlone were detrained at Blanchardstown. The artillery was positioned by the Grangegorman Medical Officer's Residency. At 3:45 pm, shrapnel shells were fired at the insurgent barricades on the bridges over the railway line to Broadstone at North Circular Road, above left, and Cabra Road. Under heavy fire, the Volunteers withdrew and some went north to join the 5th Battalion at Ashbourne. The British were now able to complete their northern cordon from Parkgate to North Wall.

Left: Broadstone Station, headquarters of the MGWR. The Volunteers hadn't occupied it on Monday, as originally planned. Daly sought to remedy this the next day, but the unit he sent was repulsed by rifles and machine guns of the Royal Dublin Fusiliers, who had occupied the station during the night.

Daly moved his headquarters to the Father Mathew Hall (left) on Church Street on Tuesday morning.

*Above: the burnt-out Linenhall Barracks. At midday on Wednesday, the Volunteers blew a charge at the wall and the army pay clerks within surrendered. Unable to hold it, the Volunteers set it on fire – it burnt for days.*

*Meanwhile, bullets began to rain on the Four Courts, from high points like the bell-tower of Christ Church Cathedral (right).*

*Boland's mills, around 1916, left, and as seen from the Grand Canal dock in the 1980s, middle left. Eamon de Valera's 3rd Battalion assembled at Earlsfort Terrace. He had planned to establish sixteen posts south of the Liffey, but his initial complement was only around 120 men. (Cumann na mBan were not present at Boland's – accounts differ as to whether de Valera had intended this.)*

*Just after noon on Monday, they occupied a wide area around their base at Boland's bakery. They established control in various places including the mills, gas works and railway workshops. The railway line, high above the streets, south-east from Westland Row Station, formed a central and strategic spine. Other outposts were set up around Mount Street Bridge.*

*De Valera was concerned about the well-being of the Volunteers under his command, and, as it turns out, for animal welfare. On Tuesday he told those of his command who were under 18 to go home. He ordered a Volunteer officer to ensure that the bakery dray horses were looked after. He also arranged for the release of animals from the nearby Cats' & Dogs' home.*

*Left: map of the 3rd Battalion area.*

*Much of the area has been 'developed' out of recognition. The towering Treasury building, above, is a rework of the successor to Boland's bakery, which had been built on the original site.*

*Above right: looking north-west, a 1950s view of Boland's bakery at Grand Canal Place. The malt-house tower is on the right.*

*Right: distillery (originally a sugar refinery, converted in 1890). De Valera had ordered that a green flag be placed on a tower of the distillery, to attract British fire.*

*On Tuesday, 'HMY Helga' fired two rounds at Boland's mills. On Thursday it sailed upriver again. The log records that it fired 14 shells at a distillery building. The green flag ruse had worked.*

*Below: Commandant Eamon de Valera*

*Volunteers seized Westland Row Station, above, on Monday. They stopped the 12:15 pm train to Kingstown, ignoring the outrage of the Station Master. They ripped up the tracks and damaged signalling equipment.*

*Left: at the heart of the 3rd Battalion territory – the Dublin & South Eastern Railway (D&SER). Railway workshops are on the left and an engine shed to the right; the malthouse tower, and the malthouse (connected by footbridge) are in the background.*

*Above: a building housing gas distribution valves at the gas works (since demolished), by Grand Canal dock. On Monday, mindful of the risk of causing fires, de Valera had ordered that the gas supply to the city be cut off.*

*Right: Beggars Bush Barracks (dating from 1827) was a strategic point in the south-east of the city. De Valera was fearful of an attack from the barracks, only lightly manned on Easter Monday, and ordered a barricade to be built at Clanwilliam Place, facing Mount Street.*

*Above: a curvilinear view of Northumberland Road. No. 25 is centre right (blue door), at end of terrace. Mount Street Bridge is at the end of the road to the right.*

*A unit of the 3rd Battalion, under Lieutenant Michael Malone, had been assigned to take over buildings around the Mount Street area, to command the approaches from Kingstown, where (correctly, as it turned out) British reinforcements were expected to disembark.*

*Volunteers moved into No. 25 Northumberland Road, vacated by its residents, nationalist sympathisers. Others occupied the nearby school and parochial hall, both of St Stephen's (the 'Pepper Canister') Church of Ireland parish.*

*Left: St Stephen's Parochial Hall.*

*Right: The former St Stephen's School, now a hotel.*

*Volunteers set up in Clanwilliam House on the corner of Lower Mount Street. This three-storey house commanded the bridge over the Grand Canal. At around 4 pm on Monday, a veteran defence force, the 'GRs' ('Georgius Rex', but in true Dublin style, nicknamed 'the Gorgeous Wrecks') marched back to Beggars Bush Barracks from exercises in the Dublin mountains. Although 120 strong, they had a few rifles, but no ammunition. The main party marched up Shelbourne Road and were fired on from Volunteer positions on the nearby railway bridges and embankment. They scrambled to reach the barracks.*

*Right: map of the area.*

*The other section of the GRs came up Northumberland Road and encountered a hail of fire from No. 25. Four died. The survivors, on reaching the barracks, clambered onto roofs and returned fire.*

*Left: General Maxwell congratulating the GRs after the Rising.*

*Middle left: view up Haddington Road, (Beggars Bush Barracks in the middle distance), from South Lotts railway bridge. The Volunteers were able to snipe on the barracks from here. They also occupied a position immediately opposite the barracks.*

*Troops were hastily mobilised in Britain to quell the rebellion. The first trains carrying the Sherwood Foresters (a regiment of the 59th Division) left Watford early on Tuesday. Below left: troops on one of the ships that sailed from Liverpool to Kingstown.*

*Loyal welcome: on arrival on Wednesday morning, the officers enjoyed breakfast at the Royal St George Yacht Club, below.*

*Some troops, on arriving at Kingstown (harbour, right) thought they were in France. At around 10:30 am the Sherwood Foresters headed towards Dublin in two columns, one via Ballsbridge, the other inland via Stillorgan. After midday, as the Ballsbridge column came near Carrisbrooke House (at the junction of Pembroke and Northumberland Roads, right) they were sniped on from nearby republican positions. The troops fired at the empty house, (previously abandoned by Volunteers from south Dublin) and seized it.*

*As the Sherwood Foresters continued along Northumberland Road a volley rang out from No. 25, below right, occupied by just two Volunteers (Lieutenant Malone had sent home two youths). Ten soldiers fell, including Captain Dietrichsen, below, who was killed. In another charge on No. 25, they were again cut down by heavy fire from the house as well as from nearby positions and Clanwilliam House.*

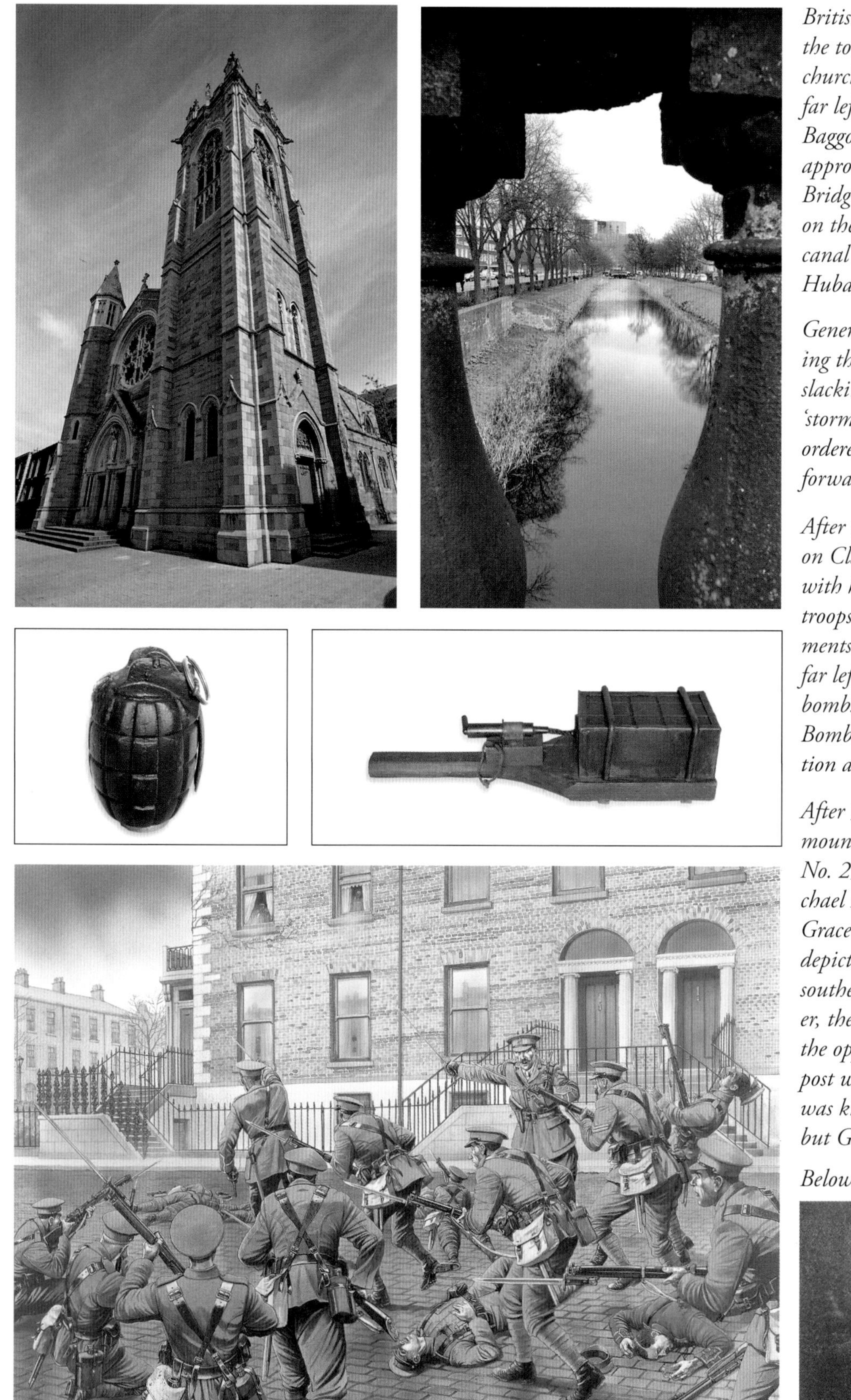

*British soldiers set up on the tower of the Catholic church, Haddington Road, far left. Others went up to Baggot Street Bridge and approached Mount Street Bridge via Percy Place on the right bank of the canal (near left, seen from Huband Bridge).*

*General Lowe, thinking that the troops were slacking, in typical WW I 'storm the trenches' mode, ordered that they push forward at all costs.*

*After unsuccessful attempts on Clanwilliam House with heavy casualties, the troops received consignments of Mills grenades, far left and 'hairbrush' bombs, near left, from the Bombing School of Instruction at Elm Park.*

*After 5 pm, the troops mounted fierce assaults on No. 25, defended by Michael Malone and James Grace. (The sketch, left, depicts the charge in the southern direction; however, the actual attack was in the opposite direction.) The post was taken. Malone was killed on the stairway but Grace escaped.*

*Below: Lieutenant Malone*

*Above: Mount Street Bridge and Northumberland Road. An office block, looking distinctly 1970s, left, stands across the bridge on the site of the original Clanwilliam House. The Arts-and Crafts-style (former) St Stephen's School is on the right.*

*The Volunteers withdrew from the parochial hall by around 6 pm. The British charged the school and found it abandoned. After many assaults they stormed Clanwilliam House using grenades and took it after 8 pm. Several Volunteers were killed, the rest escaped. The British suffered 234 casualties in total (including four officers killed), all in one day's fighting.*

*After the fighting: troops check a car on the bridge, middle right.*

*Right: bullet holes in St Stephen's School.*

*Left: around 120 members of the 4th Battalion mobilised at Emerald Square, in Dolphin's Barn at around 11 am on Monday. They set out with Commandant Éamonn Ceannt leading one unit and Lieutenant William Cosgrave the other. Their destination was the South Dublin Union (now St James's hospital). En route, parties of around 20 Volunteers each were assigned to occupy strategic outposts: Watkins' brewery at Ardee Street; Jameson's distillery at Marrowbone Lane and Roe's distillery at Mount Brown.*

*Left: the main entrance to the South Dublin Union (SDU) from James's Street in the 1950s. With its origins as a poorhouse in 1667, the location had grown by 1916 to a sprawling complex of over 20 hectares with hospitals, churches and a mortuary.*

*Left: Ceannt is remembered here; in 1916 the sloping fields were called McCaffrey's estate.*

*Below: Watkins' brewery at Ardee Street. A plucky competitor to Guinness, this brewery lasted until 1939.*

*Right: Commandant Éamonn Ceannt. Involved in the Gaelic League, and originally from Co. Galway, he was also an accomplished uileann piper. He was at the core of the revolutionary movement – a member of the Military Council of the IRB.*

*Ceannt and his Volunteers entered the SDU from the Rialto end. They spread out through the complex – whose full complement here was over 3,000 patients and medical staff. For these positions at the south-west of Dublin, the objective was to interdict British troop movements into the city from Richmond and Islandbridge Barracks, as well as from Kingsbridge Railway Station.*

*In a rapid response to the call to relieve Dublin Castle, at around 12:40 pm, soldiers of the Royal Irish Regiment set out from Richmond Barracks. As they proceeded down Old Kilmainham, they were fired on by Volunteers deployed on the heights of McCaffrey's Estate, then open ground. The troops suffered casualties and ran for cover. A company was assigned to take positions at the nearby Royal Hospital.*

*Right: map of the SDU area.*

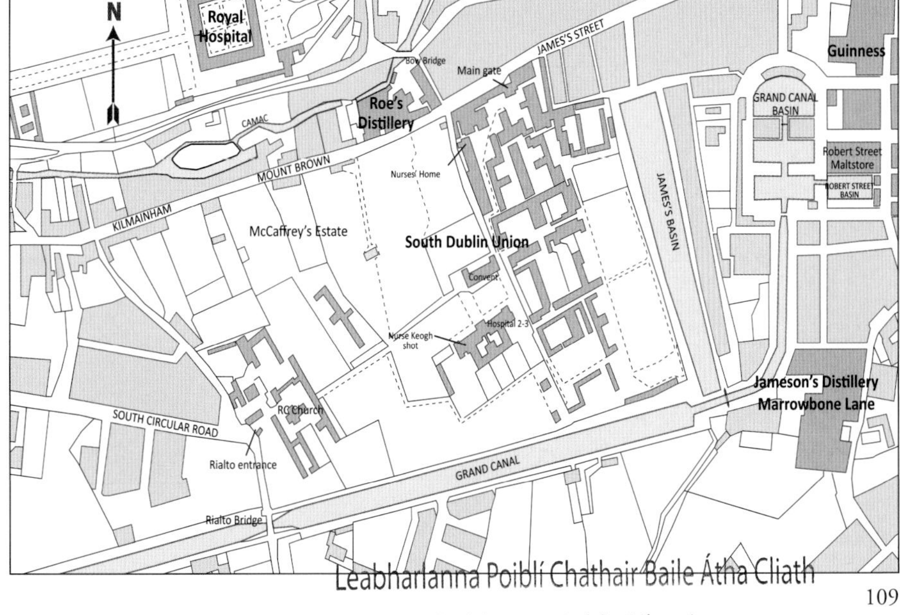

*Ceannt and his second-in-command, Vice-Commandant Cathal Brugha, had set up the Battalion HQ in the Nurses' Home, left. This imposing three-storey building was located near the front entrance of the SDU.*

*Middle left: a view of the SDU, from on high at the the Royal Hospital. The response after the initial fire from the Volunteers was not long in coming: the British laid down a fusilade of fire on the Volunteer positions, including a Lewis machine gun set up in a window of the Royal Hospital.*

*Troops were sent to encircle the SDU at the Rialto and Grand Canal ends. The British attacked a Volunteer outpost guarding the Rialto entrance. A lieutenant, leading a charge, managed to burst in though a side gate and was shot dead near the Catholic church, below left. A captain was killed as he led another charge. British fire rained down on the Volunteers, in a corrugated hut by the Rialto gate, who were now surrounded. Eventually the soldiers used a lawnmower to smash the door in. The outnumbered Volunteers surrendered. Thus by Monday afternoon the British had gained entry to the western end of the SDU.*

*Right: as seen from the Nurses' Home, the Royal Hospital, Kilmainham. Machine guns high up in the building poured fire on Volunteer positions.*

*Middle right: the Jameson's distillery at Marrowbone Lane, occupied by Volunteers. Below, right: looking west, the Grand Canal viewed from the distillery, with the SDU boundary on the right bank.*

*As a party of troops advanced along the bank of the Grand Canal, outside the SDU boundary, they were fired on from the top floor of the distillery. They suffered heavy casualties, but eventually managed to gain entrance through a door in the southern boundary. By mid-afternoon, 50 troops charged through the labyrinthine SDU complex. Fired on by Volunteers from Hospital 2-3, the troops smashed into the hospital. Running battles ensued through dormitories and past startled and terrified patients.*

*As troops took control of most of Hospital 2-3, Nurse Margaret Kehoe came down a stairway and was shot dead. Below: plaque at the hospital.*

Ċun glóire Ḋé agus onóir na h-Éireann
THIS PLAQUE HAS BEEN ERECTED TO THE MEMORY OF
NURSE MARGARET J. KEHOE
*LEIGHLINBRIDGE, CO. CARLOW*
WHO DIED OF BULLET WOUNDS
RECEIVED IN THIS HOSPITAL
WHILE PERFORMING HER PROFESSIONAL DUTIES
IN A HEROIC MANNER ON EASTER MONDAY 1916.
Go ndéanaiḋ Dia trócaire uirri
ERECTED BY THE NATIONAL GRAVES ASSOCIATION
EASTER 1965.

*Above: Nurse Kehoe*

*Left: facade of Nurses' Home.*

*By Monday evening, after a series of hide-and-seek battles, the British occupied most of the SDU. The Volunteers were well established in the front area in and around the Nurses' Home. Later on Tuesday, the British headquarters ordered a withdrawal of troops from the SDU, for some 'extraordinary reason', and this 'was done under protest' according to the regimental history. From positions dotted outside the SDU perimeter, the British continued to rain down fire.*

*When, on Tuesday evening, some Volunteers went to make contact with the nearby post established at Roe's distillery, left, they found it empty. The caretaker explained that it had been evacuated, as the captain in charge thought it could not be held and they had run out of provisions. By contrast, the distillery at Marrowbone Lane held out and on Wednesday repelled a strong British attack.*

*To cater for the poor: the Mendicity Institution at Usher's Island, formerly Moira House. Right: an 18th-century view.*

*On Monday Seán Heuston led his unit of the 1st Battalion from Liberty Hall and took over the Mendicity. The position was intended to intercept troop movements heading west along the south quays (including from Kingsbridge where – as it happened – Heuston worked). And intercept they did. At around 12:30 pm Royal Dublin Fusiliers emerged from the nearby Royal Barracks, heading for Dublin Castle. Coming under fire they scattered to the side streets. The British laid down heavy return fire. The redoubt was surrounded and on Wednesday midday, troops assaulted, throwing grenades through windows. The occupants eventually surrendered and were marched off to Royal Barracks with hands raised.*

*Near right: the present-day boundary walls. Far right: Royal (now Collins) Barracks.*

*Right: map of area.*

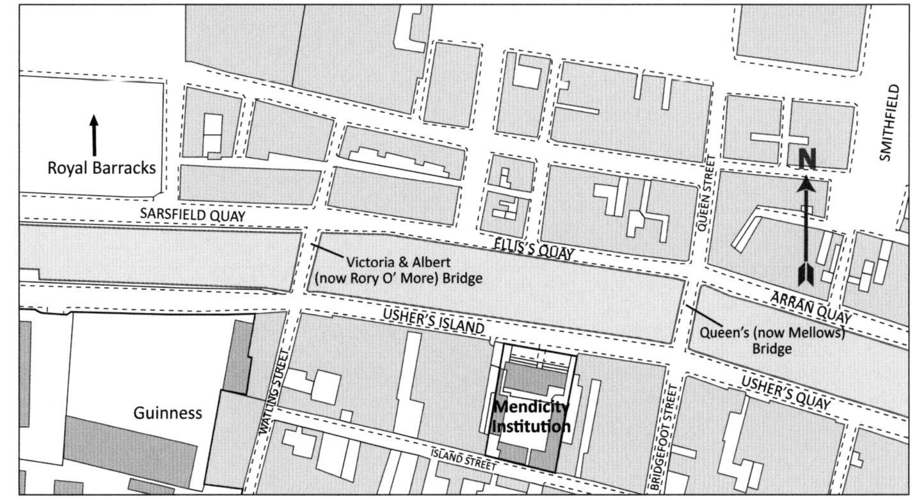


*Below: Seán Heuston*

*Left: an armoured train, made for the military by the GNR(I) in 1916. A train was also armoured in Wexford during the Enniscorthy insurgency.*

*The Rogerstown Viaduct, on the Belfast line, near Donabate, had three wrought-iron lattice-girder spans of 18 metres (left, prior to renewal). Lieutenant Charles Weston of the 5th Battalion was to place charges low on the abutments. On Monday, as there was a high flowing tide, he could only place the 50 pounds of gelignite between girders on a central pier, down line. The explosion had little effect on the open structure, merely displacing rails and timber waybeams. Single-line working was established on the other line and the damage was soon repaired.*

*Below left: the viaduct being renewed in 1985.*

*The railways escaped relatively unscathed. As news of the Rising emerged, the British, understanding the strategic advantage of railways, dispatched reinforcements by train to Dublin. On Monday a troop train went via the Phoenix Park tunnel to the North Wall. The LNWR Station, below, was occupied.*

*There were a few attempts on railway bridges, track and signals. There was minor damage, easily and quickly repaired.*

Dublin Metropolitan Police Telephone.

No. of Message | Date 191
Station of Origin | Received at
Sent at
From | To

*Near right: DMP message to the GNR(I), alerting them to the fact that 'the middle arch bridge, sloblands Fairview has been blown up'. In reality, it was a charge placed in a hole under the tracks, and was unsuccessful.*

*Above far right: the track was damaged by an explosion at Blanchardstown on Tuesday morning and this cattle special was derailed.*

*A train of the GS&WR was derailed by local Volunteers on the Maryborough (now Portlaoise) to Waterford line near Abbeyleix on Easter Sunday night, 23rd April. Right: commemorative plaque at the Colt Wood site, which also has an inscription stating 'First shot in 1916 Rising'.*

*The Volunteers did not attempt to seize Kingsbridge (now Heuston) Station, right. Reinforcements from the Curragh and the south were rapidly funnelled by train here without any interference. Following the alert given at 12:30 pm on Monday to the General Officer Commanding at the Curragh, 1,600 troops had been conveyed by train to Kingsbridge by 5:20 pm.*

SEE NOTICE AT BACK. Exhibit 6

**A.**

Prefix Code

POST OFFICE TELEGRAPHS.
(Inland Telegrams.)

No. of Telegram

**For Postage Stamps.**
*To be affixed by the Sender.*
*Any Stamp for which there is not room here should be affixed at the back of this form.*

Office of Origin and Service Instructions.

Words.

Charge.

Sent
At M.
To
By

*A Receipt for the Charges on this Telegram can be obtained, price One Penny.*

When a reply is to be prepaid, write the words "Reply Paid" in the space below. These words are not charged for.

TO { Garrison Commander Belfast

12 words, including the words in the address, 9D. Every additional word, $\frac{1}{2}$D.

What is situation in Belfast
Can you or fifteenth
Brigade spare troops for Dublin
if required

FROM { Military Head Quarters Dublin

The Name and Address of the Sender, **IF NOT TO BE TELEGRAPHED**, must be written in the Space provided at the Back of the Form.

(This Paper Manufactured and Printed by McCORQUODALE & CO. Limited. A. Wt. 34854-7/1160-1163.

10-5 pm 24-4-16

*Harcourt Street Station had been briefly seized by the ICA. Broadstone Station, not occupied on Monday, was taken over by the British that night. By early in Easter Week, all six Dublin railway termini, save one (Westland Row, within the 3rd Battalion territory) were under British control.*

*The British moved into Amiens Street (now Connolly) Station on Monday afternoon and established their eastern headquarters here. Late on Monday night, a train carrying the first elements of a composite battalion arrived from Belfast. As the republicans built barricades near the junction of North Earl and Sackville Streets, soldiers were placed in the middle tower, left, which conveniently commanded the vista along Talbot Street and beyond, to fire on Volunteer positions.*

*A cross-channel cable from the GPO ran through the Amiens Street Station telegraph office. With the assistance of Post Office engineers, a military telegraph line was opened to London, as well as a line from Dublin Castle to its head office, the Irish Office in London. Left: a telegram, sent from Amiens Street from Military Headquarters to the Garrison Commander in Belfast, requesting assistance.*

*Chapter 3*

# Final Stand and Surrender

Thursday – Sunday

*By the middle of the week the city was flooded by around 10,000 British troops (and more were on the way); against these were around 1,400 of the republican forces. Heavy fighting flared up at some Volunteer garrisons, while the GPO headquarters, and nearby outposts, were now being continuously raked with rifle and machine-gun fire. British artillery, which arrived from Athlone on Tuesday, began to tip the balance. On Thursday republican positions around Sackville Street were shelled. The British tightened the noose around the area by that evening. Parts of Sackville Street were in flames by Thursday evening. By mid-day on Friday the GPO had been hit and went on fire. By evening the roof was collapsing and the building had to be abandoned. The headquarter forces retreated along laneways and entered a terrace on Moore Street. Moved by the sight of civilian deaths, Pearse proposed to end the Rising. Unconditional surrender was agreed on Saturday afternoon. Nurse O'Farrell brought Pearse's surrender message to his commandants across the city. By Sunday the only prospect in sight was a march into captivity.*

*Three days into the Rising, the Volunteers had established outposts in buildings on the east side of Lower Sackville Street. Similarly, buildings on the west side of the street from the GPO and down to the Liffey were occupied, including the Hotel Metropole. The British had put in place outer cordons north and south of the river, as well as an inner line from Kingsbridge to Trinity College. Vastly outnumbering the insurgents, they began tightening the noose on the central area around the GPO, left.*

*Below left: map of the Sackville (O'Connell) Street area.*

*Below: the (second) War Bulletin, a handbill written by Pearse and printed in Halston Street, was issued mid-week. For the republican forces "nowhere... have the lines been broken through". This upbeat picture was soon to change as artillery was brought into play on the Sackville Street outposts on Thursday.*

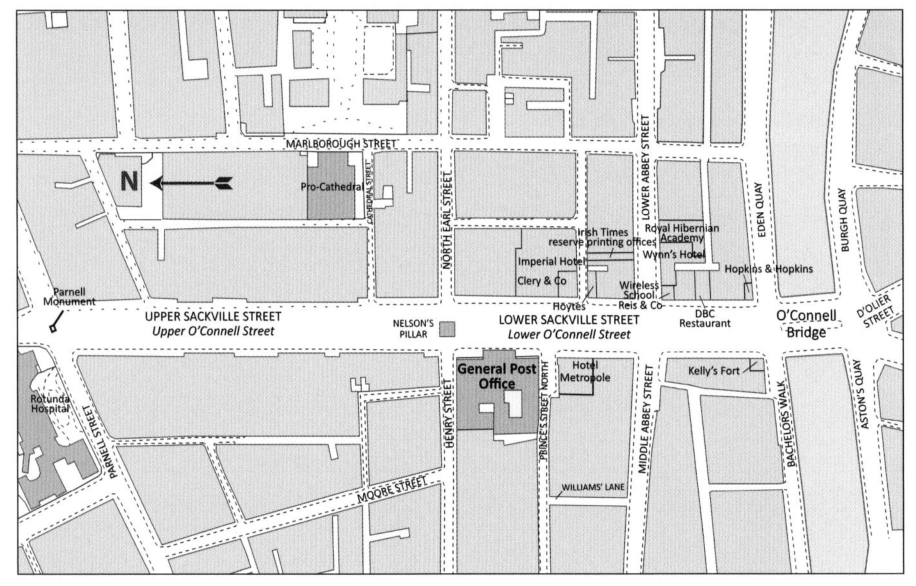

# The Provisional Government

... TO THE ...

## CITIZENS OF DUBLIN

The Provisional Government of the Irish Republic salutes the CITIZENS OF DUBLIN on the momentous occasion of the proclamation of a

**Sovereign Independent Irish State**

now in course of being established by Irishmen in Arms.

The Republican forces hold the lines taken up at Twelve noon on Easter Monday, and nowhere, despite fierce and almost continuous attacks of the British troops, have the lines been broken through. The country is rising in answer to Dublin's call, and the final achievement of Ireland's freedom is now, with God's help, only a matter of days. The valour, self sacrifice, and discipline of Irish men and women are about to win for our country a glorious place among the nations.

Ireland's honour has already been redeemed; it remains to vindicate her wisdom and her self-control.

All citizens of Dublin who believe in the right of their Country to be free will give their allegiance and their loyal help to the Irish Republic. There is work for everyone; for the men in the fighting line, and for the women in the provision of food and first aid. Every Irishman and Irishwoman worthy of the name will come forward to help their common country in this her supreme hour.

Able-bodied Citizens can help by building barricades in the streets to oppose the advance of the British troops. The British troops have been firing on our women and on our Red Cross. On the other hand, Irish Regiments in the British Army have refused to act against their fellow countrymen.

The Provisional Government hopes that its supporters—which means the vast bulk of the people of Dublin—will preserve order and self-restraint. Such looting as has already occurred has been done by hangers-on of the British Army. Ireland must keep her new honour unsmirched.

We have lived to see an Irish Republic proclaimed. May we live to establish it firmly, and may our children and our children's children enjoy the happiness and prosperity which freedom will bring.

Signed on behalf of the Provisional Government,

**P. H. PEARSE,**

Commanding in Chief the Forces of the Irish Republic, and President of the Provisional Government.

*Understandably, given the exigencies of an armed uprising, there was scarcely any opportunity for photographers to accompany the Volunteers. Here are two rare, albeit poor quality photographs, taken by photographic chemist Joseph Cripps inside the GPO. The image, right, portrays the miscellany of uniforms and weapons, as well as the age range, from what looks like thirty-year-olds to teenager.*

*Middle right: Volunteers with bayonets in scabbards and bandoliers.*

*At 10 am on Thursday a shell landed on the reserve printing offices of the 'Irish Times', on the northern side of Lower Abbey Street, where large newsprint rolls went on fire. The fire spread rapidly along a barricade (partly composed of newsprint rolls) to the other side of the street. A huge blaze ensued and Wynn's Hotel caught fire. The Royal Hibernian Academy, next door, was soon enveloped.*

*Right: vignettes by Charles Saurin, from the occupation of the Hotel Metropole. Left to right: reaching for the hotel master key with a bayonet; on hearing via the speaking tube that the brown meal sent up to his comrades was sawdust; a cool ICA man scans the street, nonchalantly perched on one of the Metropole's large oval bedroom windows.*

*Left: Seán McLoughlin, a member of Fianna Éireann and the IRB, had been a lieutenant under Seán Heuston at the Mendicity Institution. He made several trips with dispatches to headquarters, bringing supplies back to the 'Mendicity'. When this fell on Wednesday, he was cut off, spent the night with the Four Courts garrison and returned to the GPO the following morning. Aged 20 (a myth has grown that he was a mere 15) he caught the eye of James Connolly with his dash and decisiveness.*

*On Thursday afternoon, while James Connolly was inspecting outposts around the GPO, he suffered a flesh wound in his arm at a barricade in Prince's Street North. Returning to the GPO, he quietly had it dressed. Anticipating a British attack from the Liffey Street direction, he assigned McLoughlin and a section to occupy the 'Irish Independent' offices on Middle Abbey Street. Connolly supervised this, and had just turned to the narrow Williams' Lane, left, when he was wounded (by shrapnel, according to McLoughlin) just above the ankle. Painfully, he dragged himself along the laneway into Prince's Street. Eventually he was spotted and carried back to the GPO.*

*British troops continued to pour into Dublin. By 5 pm on Thursday the cordon around the central area was complete. Rifle and machine-gun fire poured in from all available high positions, including these south of the Liffey, like the Gothic Liverpool and Lancashire Insurance Co. building (at the apex of D'Olier and Westmoreland Streets) and down D'Olier Street from Trinity College, now a great British redoubt in central Dublin (right).*

*Right: depiction of soldiers manning an 18-pounder in Dublin. These field guns, transported from Athlone, were now in action with a vengeance. At one stage they were firing on open sights from Westmoreland Street towards positions in Sackville Street. Shrapnel shells were all that were available in Athlone at that time. Volunteer witness statements later mention 'incendiary shells', but these had not been developed for 18-pounder guns by 1916. The kinetic energy of a shrapnel shell, on impact, was capable of igniting flammable material. When the shelling of the GPO began, a shell aimed at one of the flags flying over it landed in the Vice-Regal grounds in the Phoenix Park.*

*Left: the green flag over the GPO, at the Prince's Street end, as photographed from the Hotel Metropole. A tricolour was also hoisted over the Henry Street end. More than one person claimed to have first raised each flag. The Plough and the Stars (page 27) was raised over William Martin Murphy's Imperial Hotel.*

*Below left: the green flag (now in the National Museum, having been returned by the Imperial War Museum in 1966). According to one account, it had been made in Fry's poplin factory of Cork Street. The letters were painted on a week before the rising, in the Markievicz home at Leinster Road, Rathmines. The flag remained in position on the GPO throughout the week, albeit with the flagpole tilting over towards the end. It was seized by the Royal Irish Regiment who are said to have later displayed it – upside down – in the regimental mess.*

*The Sackville Street area was a potential tinderbox, with stores of oil, paint and newsprint. On Thursday night, as fires raged, masses of oil drums, stored at Hoyte's chemists (Sackville Place corner), exploded. The frontage of Clerys and the Imperial Hotel collapsed. As outposts became untenable, Volunteers withdrew to the GPO.*

*Near right; Pearse had issued the third and final 'War Bulletin' on Thursday morning. Upbeat ("our lines are everywhere intact"), he berates the British for firing on the Red Cross. Pearse requested support for the Republic and condemned looting. He notes that large areas of the country are in arms for the Irish Republic.*

*With the intention, as with the 'War Bulletin', of boosting morale, on Friday morning Connolly issued a last dispatch, far right, to the soldiers of the 'Army of the Republic'. He (accurately) informed them that, by their achievement, for the first time in 700 years, the flag of free Ireland was floating triumphantly in Dublin City. Despite the flames around he ended with "Courage boys, we are winning...never was a cause more grandly served".*

*Right: The cover of the 'Irish Life' 1916 souvenir issue depicts the spectacular flames over Sackville Street on Thursday evening.*

*The GPO came under direct shell fire late on Friday afternoon. The roof quickly caught fire and began to collapse. The print by Walter Paget (overleaf) depicts the desperate scene. By evening Pearse and Connolly had decided that the GPO was no longer tenable and began to plan an evacuation.*

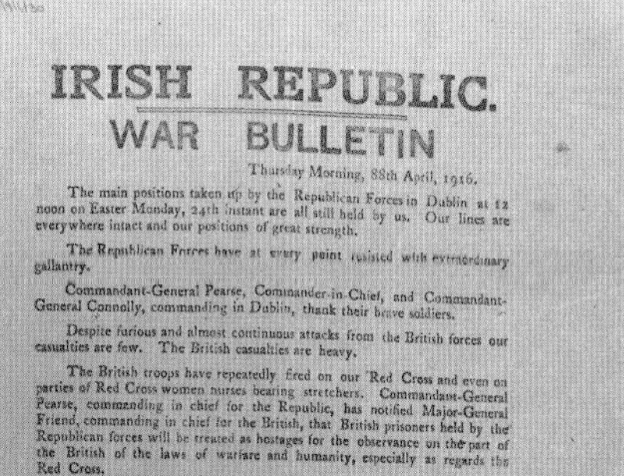

IRISH REPUBLIC.

WAR BULLETIN

Thursday Morning, 88th April, 1916.

The main positions taken up by the Republican Forces in Dublin at 12 noon on Easter Monday, 24th instant are all still held by us. Our lines are everywhere intact and our positions of great strength.

The Republican Forces have at every point resisted with extraordinary gallantry.

Commandant-General Pearse, Commander-in-Chief, and Commandant-General Connolly, commanding in Dublin, thank their brave soldiers.

Despite furious and almost continuous attacks from the British forces our casualties are few. The British casualties are heavy.

The British troops have repeatedly fired on our Red Cross and even on parties of Red Cross women nurses bearing stretchers. Commandant-General Pearse, commanding in chief for the Republic, has notified Major-General Friend, commanding in chief for the British, that British prisoners held by the Republican forces will be treated as hostages for the observance on the part of the British of the laws of warfare and humanity, especially as regards the Red Cross.

Commandant-General Pearse, as President of the Provisional Government, has issued a proclamation to the citizens of Dublin, in which he salutes them on the momentous occasion of the proclamation of an Irish Republic, and claims for the Republic the allegiance and support of every man and woman of Dublin who believes in Ireland's right to be free. Citizens can help the Republican Forces by building barricades in the streets to impede the advance of the British forces.

Up with the Barricades !

The Republican Forces are in a position to supply bread to the civil population within the lines occupied by them.

A committee of citizens known as the Public Service Committee has been formed to assist in the maintenance of public order and in the supply of food to the civil population.

The Provisional Government strongly condemns looting and the wanton destruction of property. The looting that has taken place has been done by the hangers on of the British forces.

Reports to hand from the country show that Dublin's call is being responded to, and that large areas in the West, South, and South-East are now in arms for the Irish Republic.

(Signed)

P. H. PEARSE.
Commandant-General.

Army of the Irish Republic
Headquarters, (Dublin Command)
28th April, 1916.

TO SOLDIERS.

This is the 5th day of the establishment of the Irish Republic and the flag of our country still floats from the most important buildings in Dublin, and is gallantly protected by the Officers and Irish soldiers in arms throughout the country. Not a day passes without seeing fresh postings of Irish Soldiers eager to do battle for the old cause. Despite the utmost vigilance of the enemy we have been able to get in information telling us how the manhood of Ireland, inspired by our splendid action, are gathering to offer up their lives if necessary in the same holy cause. We are here hemmed in because the enemy feels that in this building is to be found the heart and inspiration of our great movement.

Let us remind you what you have done. For the first time in seven hundred years the flag of a free Ireland floats triumphantly in Dublin city

The British Army, whose exploits we are for ever having dinned into our ears, which boasts of having stormed the Dardenelles and the German lines on the Marne, behind their Artillery and Machine Guns are afraid to advance to the attack or storm any positions held by our Forces. The slaughter they suffered in the first few days has totally unnerved them and they dare not attempt again an Infantry attack on our positions.

Our Commandants around us are holding their own.

Commandant Daly's splendid exploit in capturing Linen Hall Barracks we all know. You must know also that the whole population both Clergy and Laity of this District are united in his praises.

Commandant MacDonagh is established in an impregnable position reaching from the walls of Dublin Castle to Redmond's Hill, and from Bishop Street to Stephens Green.

(In Stephens Green, Commandant Mallin holds the College of Surgeons one side of the Square, a portion of the other side, and dominates the whole Green and all its entrances and exits.)

Commandant De Valera stretches in a position from the Gas Works to Westland Row holding Boland's Bakery, Boland's Mills, D. & S. E. Railway Works and domination of Merrion Square.

Commandant Kent holds the South Dublin Union and Guinness's Buildings to Marrow Bone Lane and controls Jaimeson Street and district.

On two occasions the enemy effected a lodgment and were driven out with great loss.

The men of North County Dublin are in the field, have occupied all the Police Barracks in the district, destroyed all the Telegraph system on the Great Northern Railway up to Dundalk, and are operating against the trains of the Midland and Great Western.

Dundalk has sent 200 men to march on Dublin and in the other parts of the North our Forces are active and growing.

In Galway, Captain Mellows fresh from his escape from an Irish Prison is in the field with his men. Wexford and Wicklow are strong and Cork and Kerry are equally acquitting themselves creditably. (We have every confidence that our allies in Germany and our kinsmen in America are straining every nerve to hasten matters on our behalf.)

As you know, I was wounded twice yesterday and am unable to move about, but have got my bed moved into the firing line and with the assistance of your Officers will be just as useful to you as ever.

Courage Boys, we are winning and in the hour of our victory let us not forget the splendid women who have every way stood by us and cheered us on. Never had a man or women a grander cause; never was a cause more grandly served.

Signed.
JAMES CONNOLLY,
COMMANDANT GENERAL,
DUBLIN DIVISION.

*Above: armoured lorry at Inchicore, 1916. In what appears to be a curious case of redaction, people in the bottom middle and right have been excised from the photo, issued in 1951.*

*Five Daimler flatbed lorries, provided by Guinness, were armoured for the military at the Inchicore Works of the GS&WR. Three of these had locomotive smoke boxes fitted. Gun slits were cut, with some decoy slits painted on to confuse snipers. Entry was via a smoke-box door at the end. Left: armoured vehicle at Upper Sackville Street, after Easter Week.*

*Right: a 'smoke-box' armoured lorry. The Daimler cab roof, sides and front had steel plate added. Joseph Sweeney, a Volunteer in the GPO, saw one of these advancing down Upper Sackville Street on Wednesday. Using his Lee-Enfield rifle, he managed to get the range. He fired repeatedly at the driver's slit and the vehicle juddered to a halt.*

*At the beginning of Easter Week, Guinness supplied 14 petrol and three steam lorries, which, in addition to the armoured versions, were used for duties such as delivering material for barricades and military supplies. Drivers were also provided and, according to an account by a Guinness manager, dressed in khaki "as a disguise".*

*Near right: this Daimler was armoured using flat steel plates. The square construction could provide more space for soldiers.*

*Below near right: another 'square' version – this time with a protruding V-shaped prow to deflect bullets more effectively.*

*Far right: letter from General Maxwell to Guinness thanking them for the use of the lorries.*

*Overleaf: artist's depiction of improvised armoured lorries scurrying along O'Connell Bridge, as flames envelop buildings.*

Headquarters,
Irish Command,
Parkgate,

DUBLIN.

17th May 1916.

Dear Sir,

At this moment, when the lorries you have so generously put at our disposal are being returned to you, I would like to take this opportunity of thanking you personally and your firm, for the splendid spirit you have displayed in coming to our help during an extremely critical period. I can further assure you that the assistance given to us by your lorries practically saved us from a breakdown in our transport arrangements, and enabled us to get through without a hitch.

I should also like to bear testimony to the pluck and loyalty with which your drivers have attended to their lorries throughout the late rebellion. It is impossible to speak too highly of their qualities, and I consider they are an honour to their firm and to their country.

I remain,
Yours faithfully,

J. G. Maxwell
General,
Commanding-in-Chief the Forces in Ireland.

The Hon: A. E. Guinness,
St. James's Gate,
DUBLIN.

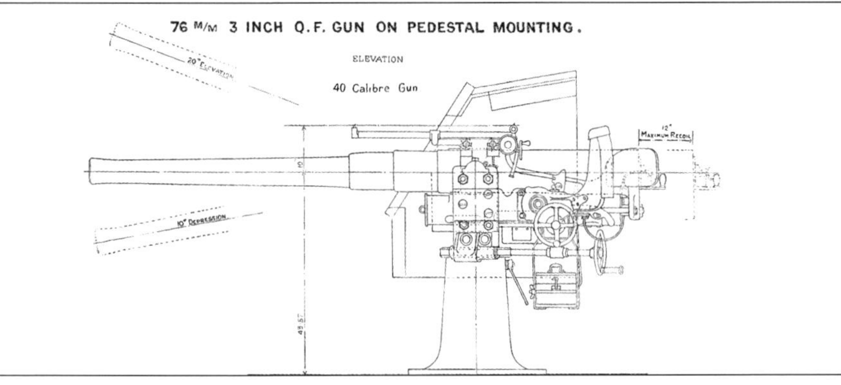

*By Thursday, the 3rd Battalion's position was being encircled. At noon a naval gun (in one account, a six-pounder from the armed trawler 'Persian Empire' and mounted on a horse-drawn coal lorry), sent 88 shells from Percy Place. In addition, 'HMY Helga' had sailed upriver and fired fourteen 12-pounder shells at a tower of the distillery., on which a flag had been planted. The deception worked, diverting fire away from de Valera's nearby HQ in the bakery.*

*Middle left: Helga's armament – a QF 12-pounder.*

*Left: Clanwilliam House, the 3rd Battalion's 'Thermopylae', in ruins.*

*Above: seen today, a 180-degree view of Commandant de Valera's world during Easter Week. His battalion was thinly spread over a wide area (including, from left): malthouse tower (the bakery was behind this); railway line; malthouse; canal docks; mills; railway engine sheds, adjacent to the tracks (replaced by the yellow office block, Google's European HQ). After Thursday, sniping was the main activity here.*
*Right: Sir Patrick Dun's hospital was opposite Boland's bakery, along Grand Canal Street. It catered for many of the casualities of the fighting and featured in the surrender by de Valera.*

*Above: Gandon's granite Four Courts became a veritable fortress in 1916, (as it also did in 1922.)*

*The British encirclement continued around the 1st Battalion positions in the Four Courts and Church Street areas. On Thursday evening, troops were deployed along the south quays opposite. Improvised armoured lorries laden with soldiers charged over Grattan Bridge and placed them along Capel Street.*

*Lancers had been besieged in the Medical Mission on Chancery Place, left, since Monday. Help was now at hand.*

*Armoured lorries rescued the Lancers. They backed up to the door of the Medical Mission and, in several sorties, evacuated soldiers, casualties and the cargo of ammunition.*

*An 18-pounder at Exchange Street on the south quays fired off several rounds at the Four Courts (one account says this was on Wednesday). The damage to the granite walls was not extensive.*

*Right: the south-eastern corner of the Four Courts complex today, and, far right, after Easter Week 1916, showing the multiple shell pock-marks.*

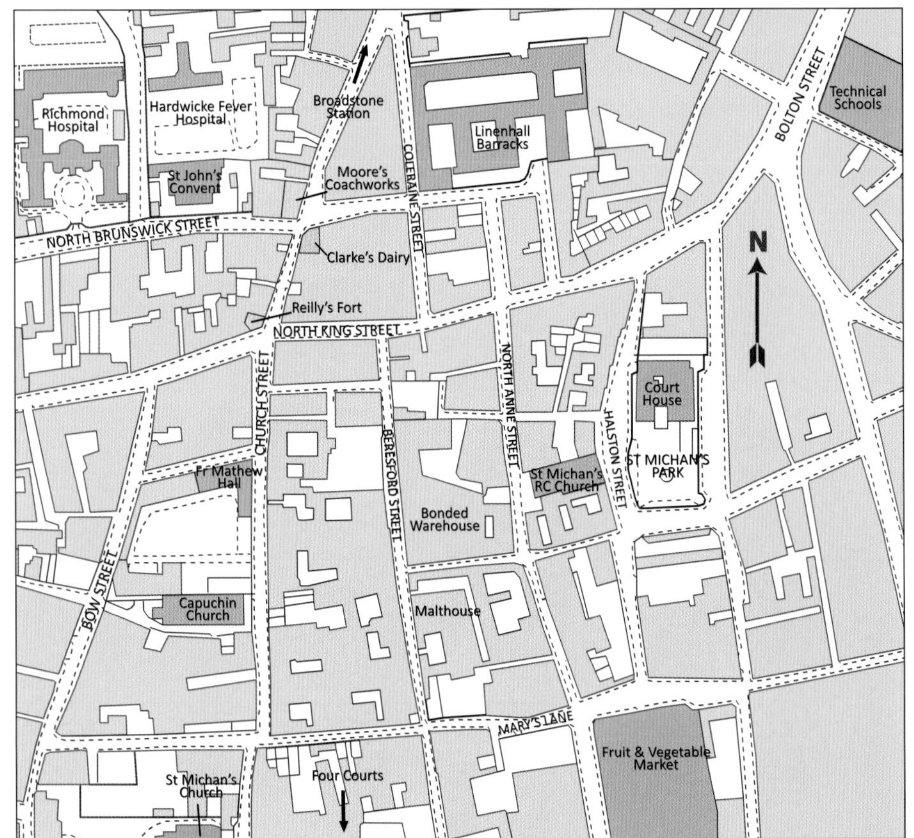


*"Few visitors to Dublin... are deeply interested in North King Street," the South Staffordshire regimental history later sniffed. The Volunteers were well ensconced in the area (then a "rabbit warren" as the history notes) around the intersection of Church Street and North King Street, occupying buildings and placing barricades. The area today, above, is much rebuilt. Much of North King Street was made up of small terraced houses, whose residents huddled within as the sniping escalated to a full battle late on Friday.*

*Left: map of the North King Street area.*

*The South Staffordshires had been assigned the task of pushing a cordon west along North King Street to join up with counterparts in Queen Street. By 6 pm on Friday they took over the Technical Schools at Bolton Street, right. The hard battle along and around North King Street was about to begin.*

*Below; Moore's Coach-works. A barricade was placed here across the street.*

*The British commanded the high points around, including the roof of Jervis Street hospital, the bell tower of Christ Church Cathedral and a tower at Dublin Castle. From the tower of Jameson's malt-house, Beresford Street, left, Lieutenant Frank Shouldice took aim and stopped the machine-gun fire from the Jervis Street roof.*
*Middle left: Reilly's (subsequently renamed Lambe's) public house at the western corner of Church and North King Streets. In a commanding position, it was dubbed 'Reilly's Fort' and was a key position during the fighting.*
*Early on Saturday morning, using an armoured lorry, troops were deposited in houses along North King Street. The lorry backed up, the soldiers exited at the rear and forced their way through doors. The soldiers began to 'mousehole' along terraces: punching holes to get from house to house. The battle continued, with few gains by the British. Later in the morning the South Staffordshires charged towards Reilly's, and they came under withering fire. Suffering many casualties, they advanced to within 30 metres of the position.*
*Far left: found in North King Street, a US-made Savage semi-automatic pistol. Near left: drawing of an armoured lorry – these proved very effective.*

*It emerged after Easter Week that, as the British troops charged into the small houses on North King Street on Friday night, they separated the men they found from the womenfolk and summarily killed many. Fifteen men were killed, two of whose bodies were hastily buried in a basement. Right: map showing names and locations of victims.*

*By 9 am on Saturday, with ammunition and food running low, the Volunteers evacuated Reilly's. With Volunteers still commanding nearby positions the area remained a killing field; fighting went on all day. By 8 pm Daly ordered all men on barricades to fall back to the Four Courts, where news came of Pearse's order to surrender. A Volunteer retrieved, under fire, the lance (captured on Easter Monday) with flag still in its position, at the intersection by Reilly's. Volunteers at Clarke's Dairy held out and didn't surrender until Sunday morning.*

*Middle right: a depiction of an insurgent barricade in Dublin. A member of Cumann na mBan and a Capuchin priest comfort a wounded Volunteer, a frequent occurrence in the Church Street area.*

*Right: barricade on the quays near Whitworth (now Fr Mathew) Bridge and Church Street.*

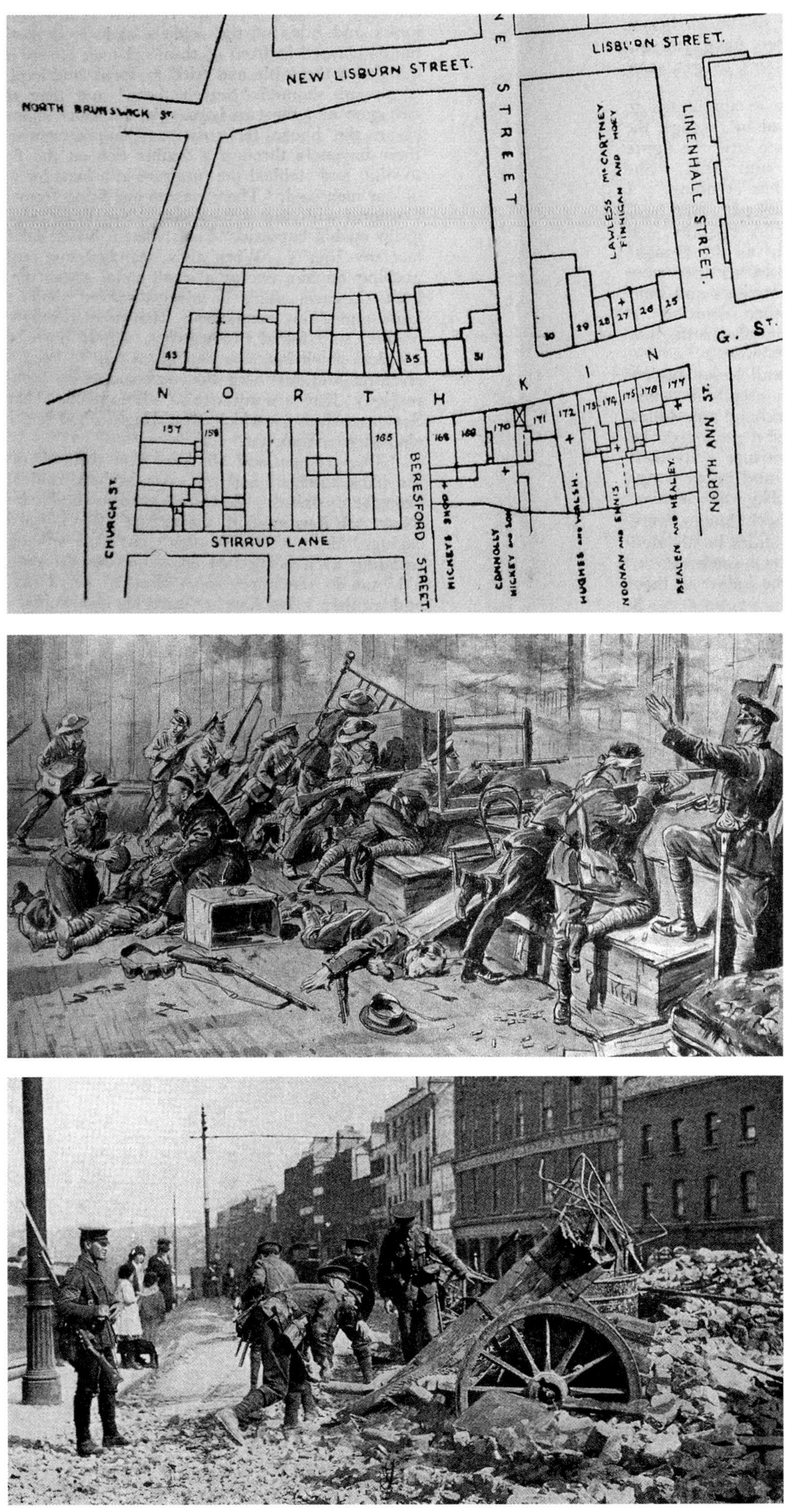

*Left: no entry to rebels – Trinity College, now a bastion. On Easter Monday, the gates were shut and a small band of the Trinity Officer Training Corps (OTC) mustered to defend the College. By the middle of the week, regular infantry and artillery poured into the College, and were billeted in rooms and squares. (Mahaffy, the Provost, complained that the horses were eating the shrubs.) This grove of academe, in the heart of the city, had been transformed into a staging post on a grand scale for the British military.*

*Left: troops arrayed around Front Square, as a convoy of wagons clatter out through Front Gate. On Wednesday, two 18-pounder guns were brought to Tara Street, from where (in tandem with the 'Helga' 12-pounder) they bombarded Liberty Hall. On Thursday two guns were wheeled out the Brunswick (now Pearse) Street gate to D'Olier Street (and later to Westmoreland Street and beyond) to shell the republican positions in Lower Sackville Street.*

*Far left: 'in Trinity College grounds; tending the grave of a fallen comrade' ran the caption. Near left: memorial to Private Arthur Smith, of the 4th Hussars, in the College today, on the boundary wall, near the Usher Library.*

*The high roofs and windows of Trinity College were a perfect platform for riflemen. Several Australian and New Zealand soldiers were in Dublin, either on leave or convalescing. On Monday they rallied to arms and joined the OTC positions in Trinity. Some had experience of Gallipoli. Sniping is a powerful technique, much advanced during WW I – it keeps the enemy pinned down and is very demoralising. The first victim was an easy target: a young Volunteer, hit as he cycled past the University on Monday. Later on, machine-gun and rifle fire was concentrated on Lower Sackville Street. Right: on high at TCD, a marksman's view up Dame Street.*

*Clockwise from near left, soldiers in Trinity: the pipers' band of the OTC; ablutions; a group outside their 'canteen' and a field kitchen.*

*There was an outpouring of loyal celebration after Easter Week. Cups (below) were presented to members of the OTC – and cups were also sent to the New Zealanders.*

*Left: surrounded by pashas and princes, General Sir John Maxwell at his farewell reception in Cairo in March 1916. A typical product of the colonial British Army, he had fought in Sudan and in the Boer War. He was in charge of the forces in Egypt when the Turks attacked in early 1915. There was criticism of Maxwell's defences at Suez, and there had been suggestions he had not adequately supported the Gallipoli campaign. He was superseded, and returned to Britain. At the outbreak of the rebellion, Maxwell, being 'available', was appointed as GOC of the forces in Ireland. He arrived at the North Wall at 2 am on Friday, 28th April. With buildings in central Dublin on fire, he headed for the Royal Hospital in Kilmainham, where he ordered an immediate advance on Sackville Street.*
*Above left: as British troops established their cordons and steadily advanced on republican positions, they too built barricades. Carts and drays were favourite components.*
*Mid page, left: British barricade at Townsend Street.*
*Towards the end of Easter Week, the city was under tight security and locked down. Troops search a motor car, far left, and ask priests for papers, near left.*

*Right: British troops assemble during Easter Week. As the week progressed, both the Dublin garrison, and the forces brought in from elsewhere, were an eclectic mix: cavalry, artillery and infantry from all over Ireland. Troops from the 59th Divison arrived in Dublin from Britain during Easter Week and elements of the 60th Division arrived in Cork. The momentum of reinforcement continued; contingents arrived just after the Rising. A brigade of artillery was unloaded at Kingstown on Saturday. Seven state-of-the-art Rolls Royce armoured cars were sent to Ireland in May.*

*Middle, right: the twin-arched underbridge of the GNR(I) over Clontarf Road. Soldiers man a barricade, made of sandbags. The machine gunner sits by his Vickers. The ladder behind allows access to their colleagues positioned on the railway line above.*

*Below right and far right: posed photographs showing an array of rifle barrels to the front, troops to the rear, at this barricade of beer barrels on the quays.*

*Below: Lee Enfield rifles and a Lewis machine gun fortify this barricade.*

*Far left: Lieut-Col Oates on right. Oates was ordered by General Lowe to move the 2/7th and 2/8th Sherwood Foresters to the Royal Hospital, Kilmainham. On Thursday 27th April, as they proceeded through the Rialto area, they came under fire from the SDU and other positions and halted by Rialto Bridge. Oates handed over command for an assault on the SDU to Major Sir Francis Fletcher Vane, near left, of the Royal Munster Fusiliers, who had arrived with reinforcements from Portobello Barracks.*

*Dublin-born, Major Vane had a colourful career. He lost his position as a military judge in South Africa for perceived pro-Boer views. He helped establish the Boy Scouts (but fell out with Baden-Powell) and also supported the suffragettes. He came back to the colours as a recruiting officer at the beginning of WW I. He had alerted Kitchener to the scandal of Bowen-Colthurst's murderous rampage during Easter Week (page 89). This honourable officer's career suffered as a consequence: in May 1916, he had to leave the army once more.*

*Troops came under fire on Thursday at Rialto Bridge, left. In 1916, this road bridge was over the Grand Canal, (now filled in and used as a Luas light rail line.)*

*Right: sketch of a Volunteer in position at Marrowbone Lane. The Volunteer garrison at Jameson's distillery, Marrowbone Lane, south-east of the SDU, was under Captain Con Colbert, who had moved his section from Watkins' brewery, Ardee Street, on Wednesday. It had been under continuous sniper fire from British positions in streets to the south of Guinness brewery. On Wednesday troops had made an assault along the canal bank, which had been countered by accurate sniper fire from the distillery. An attack was repelled on Thursday and British sniper fire continued on Friday. The garrison had grown during the week to about 100 Volunteers and 40 members of Cumann na mBan.*

*Right: the front of the 18th-century three-storey Nurses' Home in the SDU. This tall granite building proved to be an effective bastion during the battle here, where Ceannt had established the HQ of his 4th Battalion. On Tuesday an improvised flag bearing a green harp was hoisted above the building, and – predictibly – drew British fire. On Thursday the lobby and staircase just inside the front door saw the heaviest fighting of the SDU Easter events.*

*Left: convent. Entering the SDU, the troops, directed by Vane, advanced through the maze of buildings. He later wrote: "everything was bizarre...we advanced through a convent where the nuns were all praying and expecting to be shot... then through the wards of imbeciles...all shrieking". The advance towards the Nurses' Home was difficult: the troops had to run the gauntlet of rifle fire. In the meantime, machine guns from the Royal Hospital poured fire on the Volunteers in the home (now outnumbered by their attackers by a ratio of over three to one).*

*Eventually the British surrounded much of the area around the Nurses' Home. After an unsuccessful frontal assault, the troops entered the long low building adjoining the home, left, which housed wards for the elderly. Moving along corridors, they reached the end wall and punched a hole through. As soldiers crawled into the entrance lobby of the home, they were spotted by a Volunteer at a large barricade on the landing. The first soldier was shot dead. Fire was returned. Around the lobby, chaotic scenes ensued, to the sound of rifle fire and exploding grenades.*

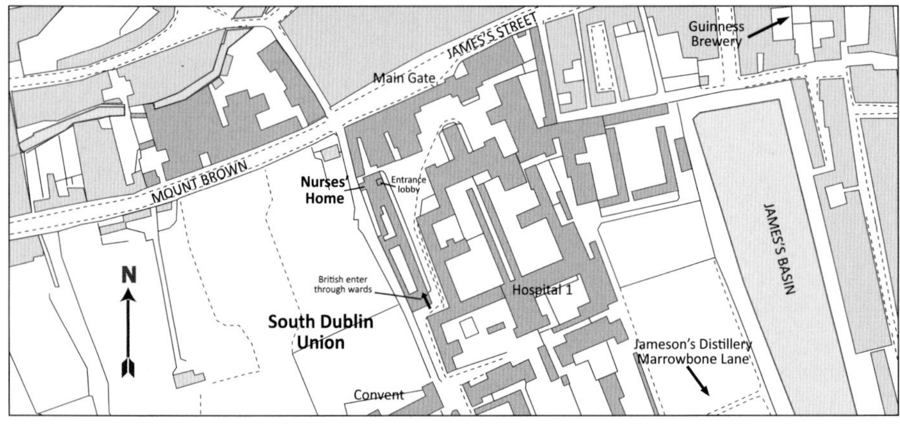


*Left: map of the area around the SDU Nurses' Home*

*Scene of Brugha's extraordinary heroism: the lobby, stairs and landing of the Nurses' Home as it was in the 1950s, above; and today, above right.*

*The Volunteers on the landing, hearing shouts, mistakenly thought they were orders to retreat, and withdrew. Vice-Commandant Cathal Brugha (bust, right) had been on the second floor. Not having heard the shouts, he went down the stairs, and was badly wounded by shrapnel from a grenade. He dragged himself to the barricade and fired an intense barrage from his Mauser C96 semi-automatic pistol. Realising that Brugha was managing to hold the position, the Volunteers mustered and as they returned to the Nurses' Home, they heard him singing 'God save Ireland'. Under the new assault, the British withdrew.*

*Hygieia (daughter of the Greek god of medicine) on the roof of the Royal College of Surgeons in St Stephen's Green (left). During the latter half of Easter Week, Michael Mallin, Countess Markievicz and the rest of the Citizen Army were well secured in the College and adjacent buildings. There was a continuous exchange of fire, but the British never mounted an assault. The rebels sought best positions on the roof and took aim at the British on the other sides of St Stephen's Green.*

*When the exhausted ICA rushed into the College on Tuesday, they lay down to sleep in the lecture rooms, trying to ignore the dissected body parts preserved in formaldehyde in adjacent rooms, a 'memento mori', considering their present situation.*

*In one large room full of portraits, one young man cut the canvas of this painting of Queen Victoria into shreds, to use as leggings. An angry Mallin ordered him to stop. Above, near left: the remains of the painting, after Easter Week.*

*Above far left: the detritus in the aftermath of the surrender.*

*Left: the sign says 'live bombs': a collection of improvised bombs, found in the College afterwards.*

*The College was under heavy fire from British position. This included from the upper windows of the Shelbourne Hotel (right) where a Vickers machine gun was positioned, as well as a Lewis machine gun in the United Services Club. The British advanced along St Stephen's Green South and mounted another Lewis on the roof of University Church.*

*On Thursday a party was assigned to occupy Russell's Hotel (now demolished) at the corner of Harcourt Street to counter these southern advances. They came under heavy fire while underway. An ICA man was shot dead and Margaret Skinnider was seriously wounded. She was carried back to the College.*

*An ICA man discovered that a British sniper was operating from a window in a shop along the Green, dressed as a woman. He took aim and shot him.*

*As the week progressed, for the ICA ensconced in their static position, lack of food became the main problem. They were hungry and even began tunnelling to a nearby pastry shop in search of sustenance.*

*Far right: bullet holes can still be seen all over the facade of the College. Near right: a brass fingerplate impacted by a bullet, in a College room.*

*As it turned out, the 2nd Battalion position at Jacob's biscuit factory, large and impregnable, did not much affect the military outcome. The British initially concentrated on establishing their inner and outer cordons across Dublin. By mid-week General Lowe had decided to leave positions like Jacob's alone and concentrate on capturing important strategic locations like the Four Courts and the GPO. Firing continued, however, from roofs and the high tower at the factory, left. In turn the British shot at the Volunteers here from high positions such as the Bermingham Tower in Dublin Castle.*

*By the end of the week, the rebels in Jacob's were tired of their diet of biscuits and were missing 'real' food. In an odd episode, some bored Volunteers started the machinery and produced some burnt biscuits. Below: model of Jacob's machinery.*

*Above: on Friday evening the situation in the burning GPO was desperate. Shelling continued and parts of the roof were falling in. At around 6 pm, a party of wounded men, accompanied by most of the women, crawled through tunnelled walls to the adjacent Coliseum picture theatre. After sheltering there from heavy rifle fire, they eventually reached Jervis Street hospital, where they were taken into British military custody.*

*Pearse decided to move his HQ to the Parnell Street premises of Williams & Woods, confectioners. The O'Rahilly was assigned to lead an advance party down Moore Street (present-day view, top right) to push through to the new location. First he would have to attack a British barricade (middle right) at the junction with Parnell Street to the north.*

Irish Rebellion, May, 1916.
*Holding a Dublin street against the Rebels.*

*O'Rahilly, with a party of about 30 men, set out down Moore Street. They split into two sections – one at either side of the street. Rifles and machine guns opened up and The O'Rahilly, right, was hit.*

*The O'Rahilly bravely continued down the street. Charging against machine-gun and rifle fire – both devastating when channelled down a street – there was no escape: he was mortally wounded just by Sackville Lane (as depicted left).*

*He crawled to a doorway in Sackville Lane (now renamed O'Rahilly Parade), As The O'Rahilly lay dying he wrote a note to his wife: "I was shot leading a rush...I got more than one bullet I think...Tons & tons of love...It was a good fight anyhow". The note is reproduced on a bronze plaque, left, at the spot.*

*Henry Place is a narrow L-shaped laneway. In 1916 it contained warehouses, factories and tenement houses. A group of Volunteers left the GPO and entered the laneway. There are differing accounts but it seems that amid the chaotic conditions in the laneway there was confusion among the Volunteers. Some broke into adjacent premises like O'Brien's mineral water factory; there was firing on positions under the misapprehension that they were occupied by the British.*

*Left: view along Henry Place – from its Moore Lane junction – west towards Moore Street.*

*Right: a 1950s view down Moore Lane, looking south from Parnell Street, with Henry Place at the end. The GPO, by now totally untenable, was abandoned. The main party, including the wounded (with James Connolly on a stretcher), Winifred Carney and Elizabeth O'Farrell, had entered Henry Place. On this laneway, at the intersection with Moore Lane, heavy machine-gun fire came from high positions at the Rotunda hospital.*
*Seán McLoughlin (page 120), aware of the "terrific blaze of fire" at Moore Lane, later wrote: "We smashed open the doors of a mineral water place and found a motor van. I got a number of men to pull this out and we pushed it across the end of Moore Lane to screen us from view". The group were able to pass the dangerous Moore Lane intersection. Later that evening McLoughlin received his battlefield promotion to commandant. Seán MacDermott also informed him that he, McLoughlin, had operational military command.*

*Right: The 'Via Dolorosa' of the 1916 Rising. Map of the area around Moore Street, where the painful journey from the GPO began on Friday evening and ended, by the Rotunda, on Saturday.*

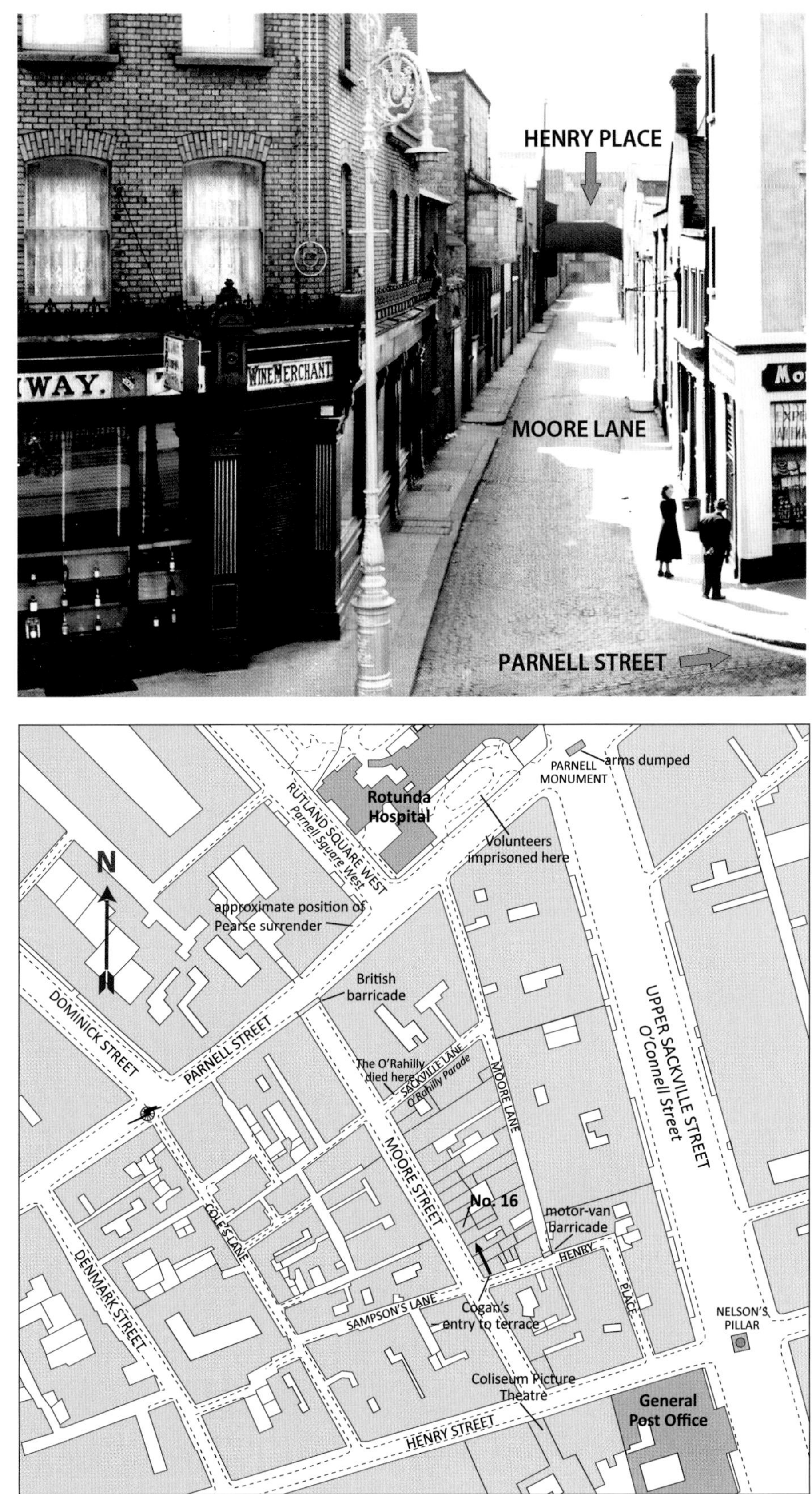

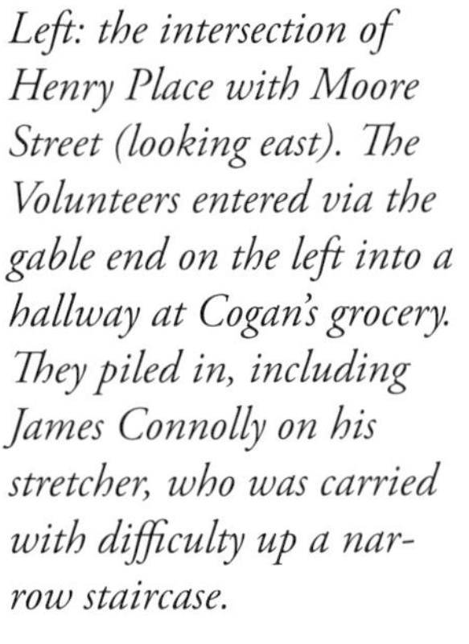

*Left: the intersection of Henry Place with Moore Street (looking east). The Volunteers entered via the gable end on the left into a hallway at Cogan's grocery. They piled in, including James Connolly on his stretcher, who was carried with difficulty up a narrow staircase.*

*The Volunteers broke through walls of the terrace of shops in the Parnell Street direction (McLoughlin, late on Friday night, ordered that while some continued with the burrowing, the rest should get as much sleep as possible.) By dawn, they had reached O'Hanlon's fishmongers (nos. 20 and 21). Later on Saturday morning they arrived at Sackville Lane, where they found O'Rahilly's body.*

*James Connolly had been put to bed in a back room of a house (No. 16 – then Plunkett's, poulterers) in the middle of the terrace. The members of the Provisional Government held a council of war here, and this unprepossesing location became the final de facto headquarters of the Irish Republic, proclaimed several days before.*

*Near left: punched-through wall, Moore Street.*
*Far left: No. 16 as it is today.*

*Above: plaque at No. 16.*

*A civilian emerged from a house on Moore Street carrying a white flag and was shot by a military volley. Other civilians lay dead on the street.*

*McLoughlin proposed escaping west to Capel Street and then to the Four Courts. Pearse discussed this with the other leaders. They decided that, to avoid slaughter among civilians and supporters, they would have to treat with the British.*

*Right: record – headed "HQ Moore St" – of the decision of the Provisional Government to negotiate. It was written by Pearse on rough cardboard, all that was available, and probably taken from a picture frame.*

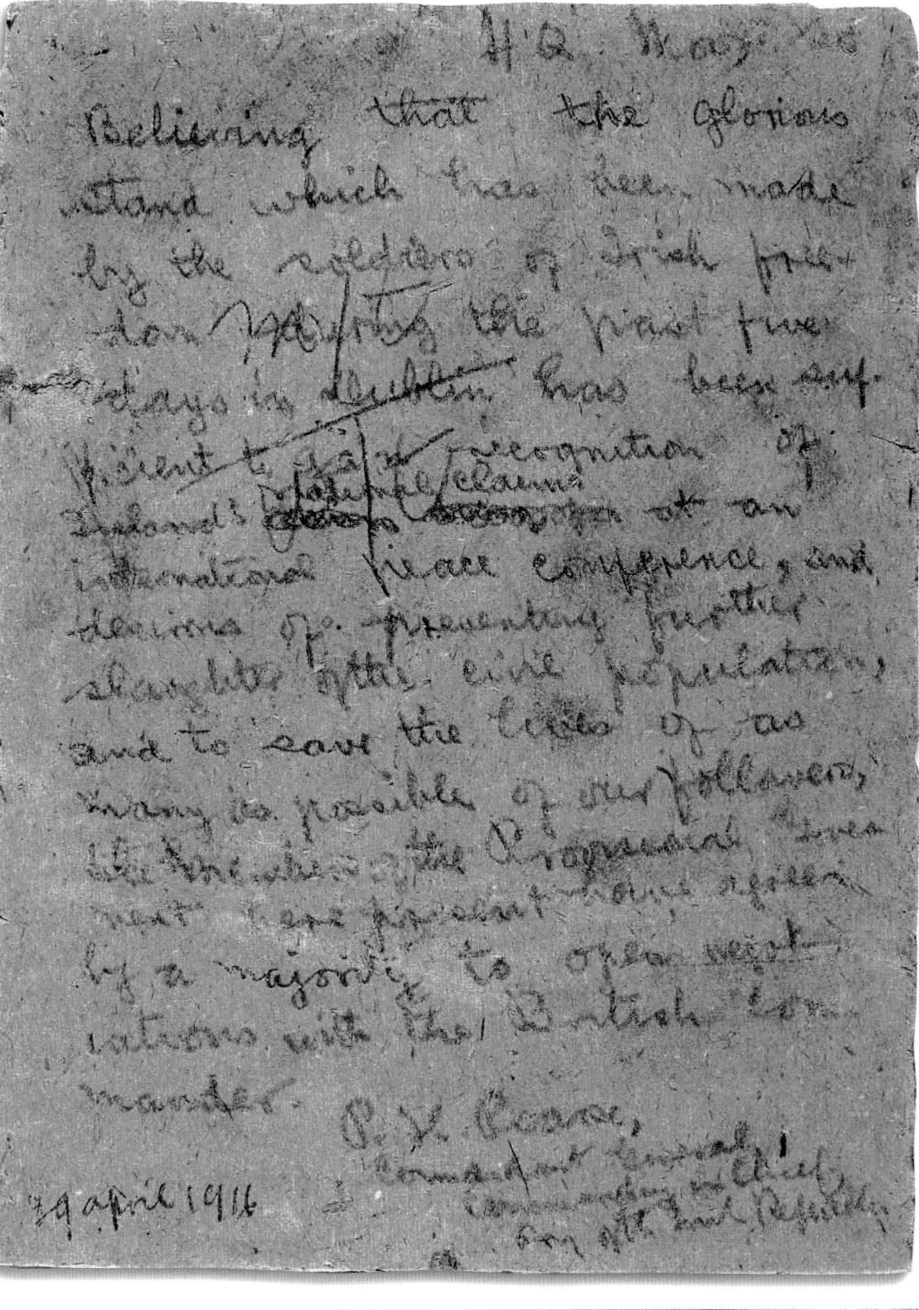

H.Q. Moore St.

Believing that the glorious stand which has been made by the soldiers of Irish freedom during the past five days in Dublin has been sufficient to gain recognition of Ireland's national claim at an international peace conference, and desirous of preventing further slaughter of the civil population, and to save the lives of as many as possible of our followers, the members of the Provisional Government present have agreed by a majority to open negotiations with the British commander.

P. H. Pearse,
Commandant General,
Commanding in Chief
Army of the Irish Republic

29 April 1916

*Right: automatic pistol (Browning 1910 7.65 mm semi-automatic, made by FN, Belgium) and leather ammunition pouch, surrendered by Pearse to Captain de Courcy-Wheeler. Small and easy to conceal, a similar model had been used by Gavrilo Princip to assassinate the Archduke at Sarajevo in 1914.*

*Above: member of Cumann na mBan, Elizabeth O'Farrell. Plaque at Holles Street hospital, where she was a midwife, left.*

*On Saturday morning the British continued shelling the republican positions in Sackville Street, unaware that they were by now empty, and were planning an assault on the GPO. About 12:45 pm, Nurse O'Farrell, wearing a Red Cross armband and carrying a white flag, walked towards the barricade at the top of Moore Street. After some incredulity on the part of the British, she was detained in Tom Clarke's shop at the corner of Parnell Street. Brigadier-General Lowe arrived by car from Trinity College, accompanied by his son – acting as his ADC – and Staff Captain, Harry de Courcy-Wheeler. Lowe told her that Pearse had to surrender unconditionally. She was escorted back to the barricade and then saw Pearse in Moore Street. She returned with a message that specified conditions.*

*Lowe rejected conditions; he would only accept unconditional surrender. Nurse O'Farrell once again went back to the Moore Street headquarters. At around 2:30 pm Commandant-General Pearse returned with O'Farrell. On the north side of Parnell Street (just to the west of the Rotunda) he met with Lowe and surrendered, handing over his sword and pistol. Lowe then suggested that Nurse O'Farrell take Pearse's surrender order to the other rebel outposts. After checking that she was willing, Pearse agreed. Pearse was taken away in a car, accompanied by Lieutenant Lowe, who was barely 18. Right: one of the defining moments of the Rising – Pearse surrenders unconditionally to Brigadier-General Lowe. Lowe's son, seen on the left, was later known as John Loder, the uxorious Hollywood actor. Nurse O'Farrell's foot and skirts can be seen alongside Pearse. On occasions they – and other references to women in the Rising – were airbrushed out. Below: approximate location of surrender, today.*

20

Part II pp 17–18

In order to prevent the further slaughter of Dublin citizens, and in the hope of saving the lives of our followers now surrounded and hopelessly outnumbered, the members of the Provisional Government present at Head Quarters have agreed to an unconditional surrender, and the Commandants of the various districts in the City and country will order their commands tp lay down arms.

original

P. H. Pearse

Dublin 29th April 1916

3.45 p.m.

copy

I agree to these conditions for the men only under my own command in the Moore Street District and for the men in Stephen's Green Command.

signed James Connolly
April 29/16

After consultation with Comdt. Ceannt I have confirmed this order, agreeing to unconditional surrender.

Thomas MacDonagh,
Commandant
30. IV. 1916.
3.15 p.m.

*Pearse was driven to army headquarters, Parkgate Street, where he met an icy General Maxwell, who was to confirm Pearse's death sentence three days later. Pearse signed the surrender order, left, at 3:45 pm. Captain de Courcy-Wheeler went to see James Connolly, who by now had been been transferred to the Red Cross hospital in Dublin Castle. As Connolly was injured, he dictated his agreement to the captain and signed it. The following day Commandant MacDonagh also signed.*

*Below: Irish-born Harry de Courcy-Wheeler, who was assigned to escort Nurse O'Farrell to the remaining republican garrisons. The Anglo-Irish world was a small one: he was distantly related to Beatrice (née Mitchell), the Irish wife of Captain Dietrichsen, killed at Mount Street (page 105). Wheeler's wife was a first cousin of Countess Markievicz (née Constance Gore Booth) and their daughter, born just before the Rising, was christened Kathleen Constance Gore, after her.*

*Nurse O'Farrell returned to Moore Street with the surrender note. The Volunteers assembled, and carrying a white flag, marched out towards Sackville Street, then wheeled left. As they approached the Parnell Monument, right, the order rang out to "advance five paces and lay down arms". They were then ordered to the front of the nearby Rotunda hospital. Others arrived, including those from the Four Courts. By 10:30 pm on Friday around 400 had assembled at the Rotunda.*

*The indefatigably brave Nurse O'Farrell, having delivered the surrender note to the Four Courts, spent the night in military custody in the National Bank, on the corner of Sackville and Parnell Streets. On Sunday, she went to the other outposts. On 1st May General Lowe wrote a note, below, stating that she had been of "great assistance" and that this may be taken into "consideration at any future date".*

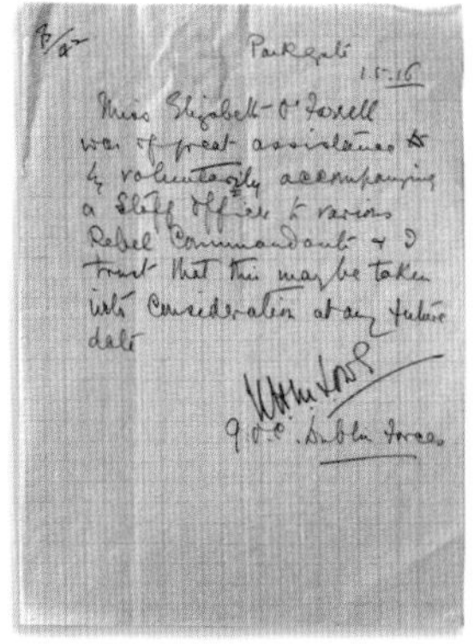

Parkgate
1.5.16

Miss Elizabeth O'Farrell
was of great assistance
by voluntarily accompanying
a Staff Officer to various
Rebel Commandants & I
trust that this may be taken
into consideration at any future
date

W.H.M. Lowe
G.O.C. Dublin Forces

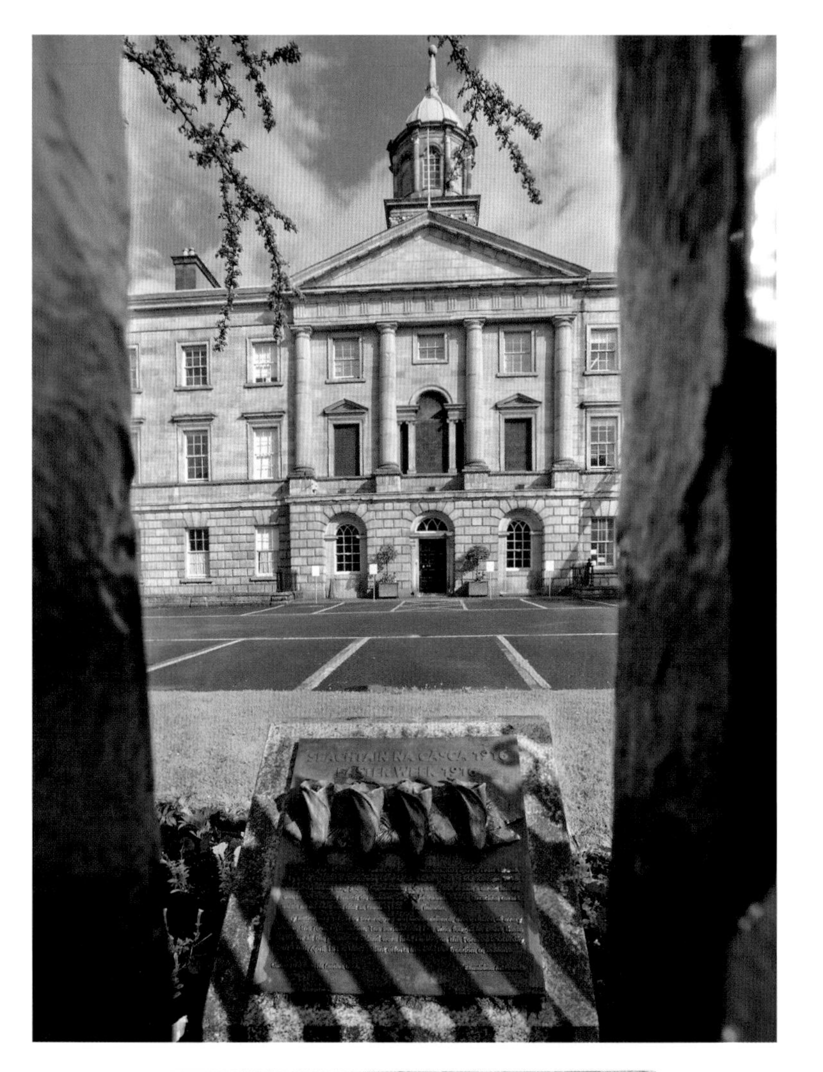

*Left: the forecourt of the Rotunda hospital. The prisoners were ordered to sit here on a small grassy strip, under military guard. A Captain Percival Lea-Wilson arrived and began to abuse the prisoners. He decreed that they could not stand up from their cramped position. He lighted on Tom Clarke: "That old bastard is the Commander-in-Chief... nice general for your **** army!" Amongst the throng of prisoners was Michael Collins, who – in 1920 during the War of Independence – had Lea-Wilson (then a RIC District Inspector in Wexford) shot. At 9 am on Sunday, after a cold night in the open, the prisoners were marched to Richmond Barracks. As they set out, Seán MacDermott, who was crippled by polio, had his stick taken from him.*

KING GOD DUTY

"Forgive them they know not what they do."

PERCIVAL LEA-WILSON,

BORN 22ND APRIL, 1887.
WINCHESTER COLL. 1900; B.A. NEW COLL. OXFORD, 1909.
CADET R.I.C. 3RD AUGUST, 1910.
D.I. FIRST-CLASS, 15TH JUNE, 1920.
KILLED 15TH JUNE, 1920.

FACTA NON VERBA

*Left: a RIC encomium to Lea-Wilson after his assassination. An interesting footnote: Dr Marie Lea-Wilson, his widow, donated a painting to the Jesuit community in Dublin, grateful for their support after her husband's death. It hung in obscurity until it was recognised in the early 1990s – 'The Taking of Christ' by Caravaggio, now restored and on display at the National Gallery of Ireland.*

To the intelligence officer —

Sir,

In the Bakery (Bolands) which my men occupied there were some ninety (90) van horses.

We endeavoured to give them food & drink — would you communicate with the manager of the mill & give him permission to get them food & drink. It would be a pity that so many

*Above: a note by Eamon de Valera requesting that the 90 Boland's bakery van horses be looked after. Nurse O'Farrell set out on Sunday morning, escorted by de Courcy-Wheeler. First she went to the College of Surgeons to inform them of the surrender. Then she was left at Butt Bridge and walked to Boland's bakery. De Valera, who did not know O'Farrell, requested orders from MacDonagh, his direct superior. O'Farrell then headed for MacDonagh at Jacob's factory. In the meantime de Valera decided to give up. He arranged the surrender through a British prisoner and the good offices of Dr Myles Keogh of Sir Patrick Dun's hospital. Above right: de Valera (arrow) leads his men to captivity at the RDS showgrounds in Ballsbridge.*

*Right: the captains and the generals – General Maxwell poses with his staff.*

*Overleaf: prisoners at Bachelors Walk en route to Richmond Barracks.*

2. AUTO ACCESSORIES Co 2
"MORGANOL" MOTOR OILS
DILLON
"MORGANOL" MOTOR GREASES
BOVRIL
RIL
TYRE
McGRATH BROTHERS
3

FURNISHER
JAMES J. SCANNELL,
AUCTIONEER & VALUER.
BACHELOR'S
4
WALK
JOHN T. DROUGHT
JAMES J. SCANNELL

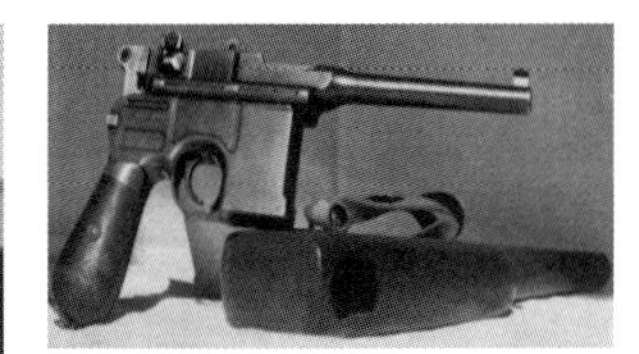

*De Courcy-Wheeler left Nurse O'Farrell at St Patrick's Park to walk to Jacob's factory where she met Thomas MacDonagh.*

*In the meantime, de Courcy-Wheeler went to the College of Surgeons. The garrison, led by Michael Mallin and Countess Markievicz surrendered (depicted, far left). Markievicz dramatically kissed her Mauser C96 (above) and handed it to de Courcy-Wheeler, whose wife was her first cousin (see page 156). Above, near left: Mallin and Markievicz under guard at Richmond Barracks.*

*There was little enthusiasm for surrender in Jacob's. MacDonagh was then driven, along with two Capuchin priests, to meet Ceannt at the SDU and inform him of the surrender order. Depicted left: in their frustration, many Volunteers destroyed their weapons.*

*Far left: days after the Rising, two dishevelled British soldiers (who had been captured) were found hiding in the ruins of the Coliseum picture theatre in Henry Street. Near left: a prisoner under escort on O'Connell Bridge.*

*Right, clockwise from top left: Thomas Ashe; map of Ashbourne area in Co. Meath; Richard Mulcahy.*

*The Dublin Brigade's 5th Battalion was commanded by Thomas Ashe. Around 60 men mobilised on Easter Monday, near Swords, armed with a few modern rifles; some had shotguns. Twenty men were sent to the GPO on Tuesday. Charles Weston had earlier been assigned to blow up Rogerstown Viaduct (page 114). As the week progressed they ranged across north Co. Dublin, and developed into a prototype of a 'flying column', attacking police barracks and seizing weapons.*

*On Friday, as they were on the point of capturing the barracks at Ashbourne, around 50 RIC arrived from Slane in a convoy of 17 cars. A firefight ensued. The Volunteers moved around the 'bocage' of hedges and fields and outmanoeuvred the RIC. Richard Mulcahy brilliantly led a bayonet charge; the RIC surrendered, suffering eight dead.*

*Right: monument at Rath crossroads.*

*Below: the 'bocage' along the Garristown road.*

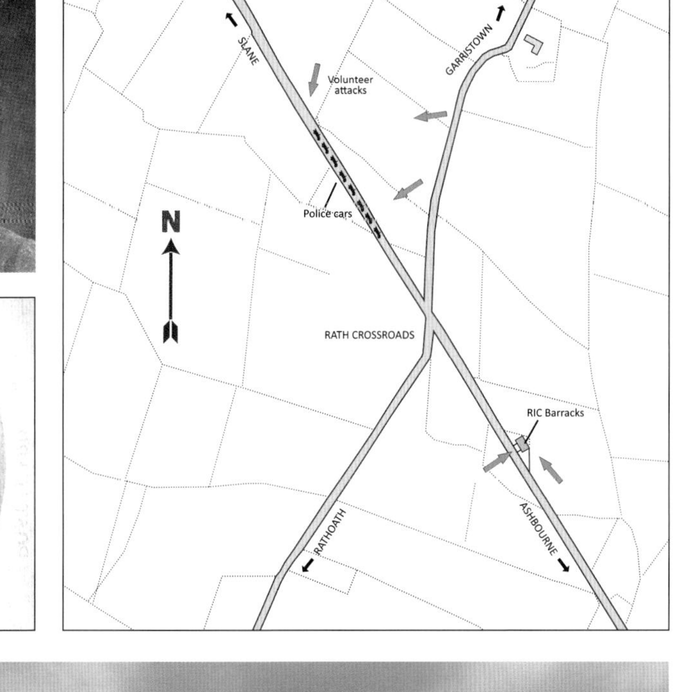

*The rising in the country has been described as 'somewhat amorphous'. The countermand; poor planning and communication; and the failure of the Kerry arms landing all resulted in confusion and wasted effort. In Louth, some of the Volunteers hadn't even heard of MacNeill's countermand. On Easter Sunday they set out. Over the week they captured arms and police and then disbanded. To a greater or lesser degree, Volunteers in Cork, Kerry, Limerick and Ulster, mustered, assembled and later went home.*

*In various parts of Co. Galway around 1,000 Volunteers assembled. Liam Mellows, above left, led a core force which marched to various places and ended up at Tulira Castle, where, by week's end, they disbanded.*

*Far left: Paul Galligan. After he returned from the GPO with news, Volunteers took over Enniscorthy on Thursday. News of surrender came on Sunday, 30th April. Two Volunteers went to Dublin to see Pearse, who verified this.*

*Above middle: note on surrender, from Colonel French. Above middle right: statue of Volunteer Commandant Seamus Rafter, in Enniscorthy.*

*Left: Wexford Volunteers en route to Kilmainham Gaol, with an officer and escort.*

*Chapter 4*

# Retribution and Remembrance

*As the republican outposts surrendered, the citizens of Dublin took stock of their shattered city centre. With Ireland under martial law, General Maxwell had carte blanche to deal with the aftermath of the rebellion – he proceeded in a thoroughly draconian manner. Field General Courts Martial were rapidly set up. The trials were rushed and lacked any semblance of justice. Leaders of the Rising, as well as less prominent figures, were sentenced to death. There was a vacuum of power in Dublin and Maxwell filled it – he confirmed sentences without any real hindrance from the unassertive Prime Minister Asquith. The executions were carried out with military expedition. The Volunteers had been jeered at as they were marched to captivity, but as the executions proceeded a shift in mood occurred. The change in public support helped propel the War of Independence that followed. Achievement of the Republic that had been proclaimed in 1916 was the principal raison d'être for the 1922-23 Civil War. Remembrance and understanding of 1916, essential to the foundation myth of the Irish state, continues as a complex source of controversy.*

*Two views of Lower Sackville Street from Nelson's Pillar after the Rising. Left: looking southwest, the GPO in ruins. Miraculously, the portico was mostly intact, but the rest of the huge complex was a burnt-out shell. Below left: looking southeast, the shell of the Imperial Hotel. The destruction in and around Lower Sackville Street resulted mostly from fire. Shrapnel shells, fired from the British 18-pounders, were the initial cause of ignition on flammable materials, then the flames spread. A shell falling on the 'Irish Times' reserve printing office on the western side of Lower Abbey Street at around 10 am on Thursday started a fire which spread and led to a grand conflagration. By the end of the week, most areas around Lower Sackville Street had been damaged by fire.*
*James Connolly is reputed to have argued that the British would never employ artillery in Dublin: a capitalist government would not choose to destroy property. This maxim proved to be wrong. General Maxwell had free rein militarily and was also unhindered by any real political restraints. Faced with insurgents embedded in a built-up area, the military single-mindedly resorted to whatever weapon was effective, in this case 18-pounders.*

*Above: from the furnace of revolution – fused fragments of metal and bullet cartridges found in the burnt-out GPO.*

*Above right: the damage as seen from O'Connell Bridge.*

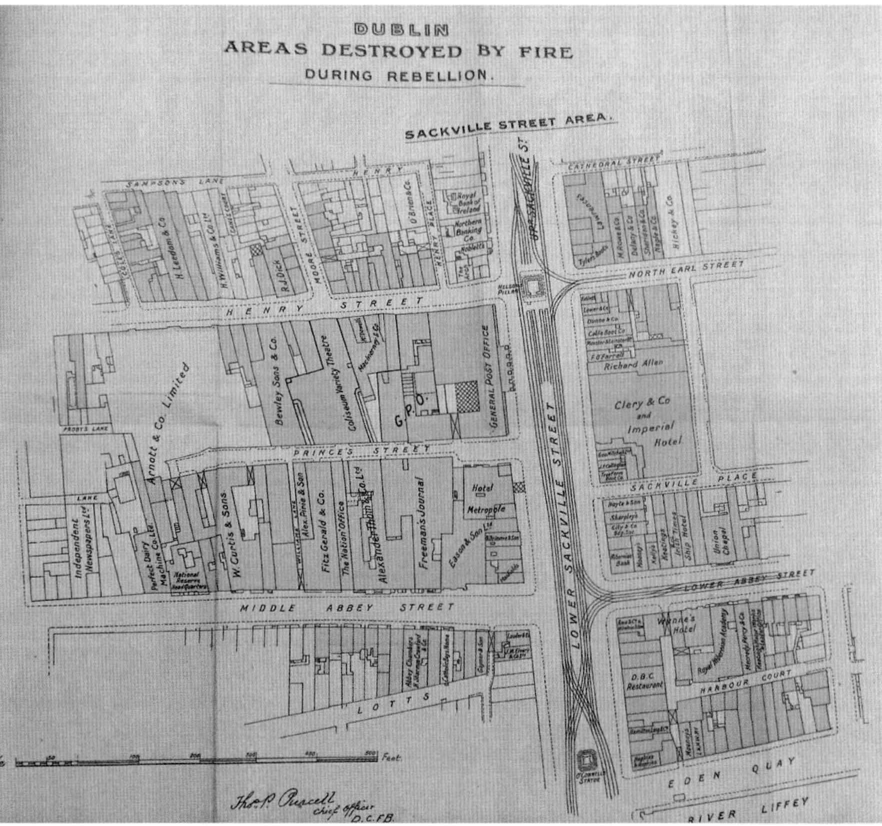


*Right: a map, prepared by Captain Purcell, head of the Dublin Fire Brigade, showing the post-Rising damage in central Dublin.*

*Below right: hard at work in the new Telegraph Instrument Room, set up on the top floor of Amiens Street parcels office. With the original telegraph room in the GPO out of action, the Post Office, moving with military-style efficiency, had commissioned the replacement facility by Tuesday 9th May.*

*Overleaf: looking northwards at the ruins of the Hotel Metropole, with the GPO in the background, and the ruined facade of the Imperial Hotel, seen through the gap to the right. The Dublin contractors engaged in removing the rubble, Messrs Clifton and Cooper, have enterprisingly erected their sign.*

CLIFTON & COOPER
CONTRACTORS

*The GPO had just been extensively – and expensively – modernised a short time before Easter 1916. Stark iron arch trusses span the rubble of the Public Office, above. The image shows "all that was left of the costly fittings" as the Post Office photographer sourly captioned it.*

*Another sour view: this photograph of the Dublin ruins from on high, above left, is captioned in the 'Great War' magazine as "The price of the Sinn Féiners' extravagant ideal." Copies of the Parthenon marbles, left, at the Royal Hibernian Academy on Lower Abbey Street, and below, in ruins. The building was designed by Francis Johnston in 1824. The upper facade has been retained in the replacement building. The 'Irish Times' printing office, opposite, shelled on Thursday, went up in flames, which spread across the street via a barricade of newsprint rolls, first to Wynn's Hotel and then to the Academy.*

*Right: devastation, looking east up Henry Street towards Nelson's Pillar. The buildings on both sides of the street were destroyed: on the right, the GPO and buildings leading up to it; the buildings at the junction with Moore Street are to the left.*

*Middle right: a view of the junction of Lower Abbey and Sackville Streets. Reis's premises (whose top floor had housed the Irish School of Wireless) at the corner has disappeared into rubble. The distinctive polychromatic (and now skeletal) frontage of the DBC restaurant, is to the right.*

*William Martin Murphy, Chairman of the Dublin United Tramway Company, later reported that damage was comparatively light during the Rising: just two tramcars, burned in the streets, and some damage to the overhead wire system. The company's distinctive HQ, described as being in 'Scottish-Baronial' style, on Upper Sackville Street escaped damage, though adjacent buildings to the south were damaged. (The HQ was demolished after being badly damaged in the fighting in central Dublin during the Irish Civil War in early 1922). Right: bullet holes in the window of a Dublin tram.*

*A kepi of the Dublin Fire Brigade. The founder of the original Dublin service had worked in the New York Fire Department and introduced the kepi, similar in style to that of a United States Army officer. Starting on Monday, Dublin Fire Brigade struggled manfully all week to extinguish fires. Periodicals published just after the Rising alleged darkly that the Volunteers had fired on the firemen, but it is likely that both sides sniped at anyone in uniform. Left: firemen at what remained of Hopkins jewellers, at Eden Quay retrieve a safe which was still red-hot – the contents were found to be intact.*

*There was a bizarre incident at the Guinness Robert Street malthouse, left, located near the SDU, where a military guard had been placed. On the night of 28th April, when a lieutenant and a night watchman entered the malthouse, the sergeant in charge had them shot, thinking they were 'Sinn Féiners'. Two more arrived; again both were shot. The sergeant was tried for murder, but found not guilty.*

*Right: in the aftermath of the Rising, W & R Jacob sent a cheque for £25 to the Capuchin Father Aloysius (who had assisted in negotiations of surrender there) in appreciation that "our Factory was spared from serious injury during...the recent rebellion". Aloysius thanked them and returned the cheque, writing that "any services that I may have rendered... were such as my duty as a Priest...(required)."*

*'Traitté de l'Église' is a modest book by a Huguenot theologian, published in Geneva in 1649 and was part of the collection of the first Keeper at Marsh's Library, Élie Bouhéreau. About an hour after the surrender of the garrison at Jacob's factory (near the library) on Sunday, a burst from a British machine-gun post in the Iveagh Buildings, around 350 metres away, shattered the window of the library, and damaged five books. Showing how a bullet can cause devastating injuries to a person, one entered the spine of the 'Traitté de l'Église' book, ripped and distorted as it moved along, right. The bullet exited, ricochetted back from the adjacent wall and hit the book a second time, below.*

ORIGINAL MAKERS OF CREAM CRACKERS, PUFF CRACKNELS ETC.
TELEGRAMS: JACOB, DUBLIN.
TELEPHONE: Nº 2588.

By Royal Appointment To H.M. the KING

LONDON DEPÔT: DOCKHEAD, S.E.
LIVERPOOL " : SCOTLAND Rᴰ
MANCHESTER " : TRAFFORD PARK.
BRANCH FACTORY, AINTREE, LIVERPOOL.

W. & R. JACOB & Cº LTD
BISCUIT MANUFACTURERS,
DUBLIN.

Please quote reference

TWB/AHH May 25th 1916

The Very.Rev.Father Aloysius,
Franciscan Capuchin Priory,
Church St.

Dear Sir,

Under a deep sense of thankfulness that our Factory was spared from serious injury during the time of the recent Rebellion, my Directors have asked me to hand you the enclosed cheque for £25, which they would be glad you would make use of in connection with the temperance work carried on by your Order.

Yours faithfully,

Thomas W Bewley
Secretary.

All communications to be addressed to the company

249

LIVRE II.

*Second poinct du propos de la perpetu[...]elle subsistence de l'Eglise, ass. qu'elle ne subsiste pas tousiours auec eminence & splendeur, mais est par fois tellement obscurcie & offusquée, qu'il est difficile de la reconnoistre.*

NOSTRE second poinct est, Que la subsistence de l'Eglise, quant à son estat exterieur, n'est pas tousiours auec splendeur & eminence, mais

TÓGADH AN LEACHT SEO I
NDÍL-CHUIMHNE AR NA DAOINE CRÓGA
A GHLAC PÁIRT IN ÉIRÍ ÁMACH
1916 AGUS A COIMEÁDADH I
NGÉIBHEANN SA HALLA SEO AR
FEADH TAMAILL I NDIAIDH AN
ÉIRI ÁMACH BHÍ NA DAOINE SEO
A LEANAS [illegible] NA GCÉADTA A
BHÍ FAOI [illegible] ANSEO I RITH
AIBREÁIN AGUS BEALTAINE 1916
PÁDRAIG AGUS WILLIE PEARSE
SEÁN MAC DIARMADA
SEOSAMH PLUINCÉAD
ÉAMON DE VALERA
TOMÁS MAC DONNCHA
TOMÁS Ó CLÉIRIGH. ÉAMON CEANNT
COUNTESS MARKIEVIEZ
WILLIAM T. COSGRAVE
MAJOR SEÁN MAC BRIDE
MICHAEL COLLINS. ART Ó GRÍOFA
EOIN MAC NEILL. TOMÁS ASHE
NOEL LEMASS. SEÁN T. Ó CEALLAIGH
AR DHEIS DÉ GO RAIBH A N-ANAMACHA UILE

*Above: plaque at gymnasium, Richmond Barracks, Inchicore.*

*Left: Searching at Tolka Bridge, Drumcondra for arms and ammunition.*

*Most of those captured were brought to Richmond Barracks. They were placed in the gymnasium, left. DMP 'G'-men' would peer through windows of the partition at the back, scrutinising and selecting suspects. Those suspected of being in senior roles were held in the barracks for trial. In the days and weeks that followed, prisoners were marched to ships on the quays and thence to internment in Britain.*

*Below, far left: in captivity at Richmond Barracks. Below, near left: en route by prison van to the quays.*

*Unlike the other leaders, Patrick Pearse and Seán Heuston were held at Arbour Hill Detention Barracks (below).*

*With martial law in force, General Sir John Maxwell, near right, was in full control. Having spent much of his career on campaign in the colonies, he now had to deal with this rebellious semi-colony. He set up a regime of punishment, untrammelled (at least initially) by any effective political control or nuanced consideration of the impact on opinion across Ireland. To deter future insurgency, his priority was to punish the rebel leaders quickly, both for association with the German enemy and for the loss of life and damage to property.*

*Field General Courts Martial were established – a simplified wartime form, quicker and with a more predictable outcome. There was no legal representation for the accused and no right of appeal. The trials were held in camera. William Wylie, a young Dublin barrister, Second-Lieutenant (the lowest commissioned rank) in the Trinity OTC, was appointed to prosecute. He was aware of the deficiencies of the procedure and is acknowledged as trying to help the accused, where possible. He was later appointed to the High Court by the Irish Free State. (Regalia, top far right). Trials were held at Richmond Barracks, middle right, and executions at Kilmainham Gaol, right.*

*The first trials were on 2nd May, of Patrick Pearse, top far left, Thomas Clarke, above, and Thomas MacDonagh, far left. All three, signatories of the Proclamation, were sentenced to death.*

*Pearse made a dignified speech at his trial. He said that "...as I am one of the persons chiefly responsible...I am prepared to take the consequences of my act, but I should like my followers to receive an amnesty."*

*Near left: under intertwined serpents, the main entrance to Kilmainham Gaol, Ireland's 'Bastille'.*

*Pearse wrote to his mother that: "Our deeds of last week are the most splendid in Ireland's history... we shall be remembered by posterity..." At a later social occasion, Major-General Blackader confided that he had just condemned to death one of the finest characters (Pearse) he had ever come across.*

*Tom Clarke, eldest of the leaders, was a veteran Fenian and the IRB éminence grise of the Rising. On the eve of his execution, he fatalistically told his wife that he was relieved to be executed, as he dreaded a return to prison.*

*Right: Clarke's cell. Kilmainham had ceased to be a convict prison in 1910. It was reopened for military prisoners. Conditions were primitive – there was scarcely any furniture for prisoners, sacks on the floor, and lighting was by candle-light or gas-flame.*

*Far right: a final testimony by MacDonagh, written at midnight on 2nd May. He affirms "I have been actuated by one motive, the love of my country, the desire to make her a sovereign independent state."*

*Near right: an urgent DMP telegram sent on 2nd May, from Military HQ to the Capuchin Fathers at Church Street stating that "the two men they wish to see at Kilmainham Detention Prison should be seen by them tonight".*

**Dublin Metropolitan Police Telephone.**

No. of Message. Date, 2. 5. 1916
Station of Origin. Received at M.
Sent at M.

| From | To |
|---|---|
| Military HQ Parkgate St | Police G Div |

Please tell the Franciscan Fathers at Church Street that the two men they wish to see at Kilmainham Detention Prison should be seen by them tonight –

Kilmainham Gaol.
Midnight Tuesday 2nd May.

I Thomas McDonagh having now heard the sentence of a court-martial held on me today declare that in all my acts, all the acts for which I have been arraigned, I have been actuated by one motive, the love of my country, the desire to make her a sovereign independent state. I still hope and pray that my acts may have for her some lasting freedom and happiness. I am to die at dawn 3.30 A.M. 3rd May. I am ready to die and I thank God that I die in so holy a cause. My country will reward my deed richly. On April 30th I was astonished to receive by a message from P.H. Pearse Commandant General of the Army of the Irish Republic an order to surrender unconditionally to the British General. I did not obey this order as it came from a prisoner. I was then in supreme command of the Irish Army, consulted with my 2nd in Command and decided to confirm the order. I knew that it would involve my death and the death of other leaders. I hoped that it would save many true men among our followers, good lives for Ireland. God grant it has done so and God approve our deed

*Pearse, Clarke and MacDonagh were all shot in the grim Stonebreakers' Yard, above, at Kilmainham at dawn on 3rd May.*

*Joseph Plunkett, Edward Daly, William Pearse and Michael O'Hanrahan, were tried on 3rd May. Their death sentence was swiftly confirmed by General Maxwell and they were executed on the 4th.*

*Hours before he was executed, Joseph Plunkett, far left, married his fiancée, Grace Gifford, near left.*

*A signatory of the Proclamation, Plunkett (portrait by Grace Gifford, right) had been at the heart of the planning of the Rising. He had visited Germany in 1915, where – together with Casement – he had sought German assistance in support of a rising by the Irish Volunteers. He had served in the GPO despite having a recent operation for tubercular glands: his neck was still bandaged.*

*Grace Gifford (who had just heard of her brother-in-law Thomas MacDonagh's execution) bought a wedding ring at a jeweller's shop in Grafton Street on the evening of 3rd May. She met Joseph in the chapel at Kilmainham, below right, at around 11 pm. With soldiers as witnesses, they married by the light of a single candle. The couple were allowed 10 minutes together in a cell full of soldiers when she returned at around 2 am. Plunkett was then shot at dawn.*

*Overleaf: executions were gruesomely simple. An officer had previously inserted a blank in a random rifle of one of a 12-man squad, who were marched into place. Along with a priest, the blindfolded and bound prisoner was escorted to the yard. The order rang out: "Ready, Present, Fire!" The soldiers were then marched away.*

*Far left: Limerick-born Edward Daly was Commandant of the 1st Battallion, involved in firece fighting in North King Street and the Four Courts. Only 25, Daly came from a Fenian family, (a nephew of John Daly, page 37). Asquith had issued a general proclamation that death should only be inflicted on "ringleaders and proven murderers". The case of the next person to be shot illustrates the fickleness of a rushed trial procedure. William Pearse, schoolteacher, actor and gifted sculptor, middle far left, had merely been a captain in the GPO. Simply being Patrick's brother contributed to the rationale for his death. Michael O'Hanrahan, above near left, part-time journalist, had an administrative post at Volunteer HQ. Only third in command at the Jacob's factory, he was sentenced to death.*
*John MacBride, (near left) never in the Irish Volunteers, had shown up and offered to assist at Jacob's factory. He was only second in command there, where there was little action. His notoriety in fighting the British in the Boer War contributed to his fate – he was shot on Friday, 5th May.*
*Capuchins who ministered to the 1916 leaders included Albert, far left, and Aloysius, near left.*

*Right: corridor of death – cells at Kilmainham, where the condemned men spent their last hours. After the first executions, a nervous Asquith (described by the historian Charles Townshend as "a famous procrastinator") told Maxwell that there should be no hasty procedure, and of the need to avoid the sowing of seeds of lasting trouble in Ireland. Maxwell was called to London on 5th May to a Cabinet meeting. However, he was effectively left to exercise his own discretion.*

*All the executed leaders met their deaths bravely. Their courage and clarity about their objectives were reflected in some of their last writings.*

*Below far right a letter from Seán Heuston to a railway colleague: "Before this note reaches you, I shall have said farewell to this Vale of Tears... Whatever I have done I have done as a soldier of Ireland..." Near right: Seán MacDermott, in his letter to the old Fenian, John Daly, states that "I have been sentenced to a soldier's death – to be shot tomorrow morning. There is nothing to say about this only that I look on it as part of the day's work. We die that the Irish nation may live, our blood will re-baptise and reinvigorate the old land."*

Kilmainham Prison
Dublin
May 11th 1916

My dear Daly
Just a wee note to bid you Good Bye
I expect in a few hours to join [Tom] and the other
heroes in a better world. I have been sentenced to
a soldier's death – to be shot to-morrow morning.
I have nothing to say about this only that I look
on it as a part of the day's work. We die
that the Irish nation may live, our blood will
re-baptise and reinvigorate the old land. Knowing
this it is superfluous to say how happy I feel. I
know now, what I have always felt, that the Irish
nation can never die. Let present day place hunters
condemn our action as they will, posterity will judge
us aright from the effects of our action.
I know I will meet you soon, until then
Good Bye. God guard and protect you and all in
No 15. You have had a sore trial, but I know
quite well that Mrs Daly and all the girls
feel ~~bound~~ [proud] in spite of a little temporary and
natural grief, that her son, & the girls, their brother
as well as [Tom] are included in the list of honours

Kilmainham Prison
Dublin
Sunday
May 7

Dear Mr Walshe
Before this note reaches you
I shall have said farewell to this
Vale of Tears and have departed for
what I trust will prove a much
Better World. I take this last
opportunity of tha[illegible] you and all
my Railway friends for the kindness
of the past years. I ask all to forgive
me for any offences which I may have
committed against them and I ask
all to pray fervently for the repose
of my soul. Whatever I have
done I have done as a soldier
of Ireland in what I believed to
be my country's interest. I have

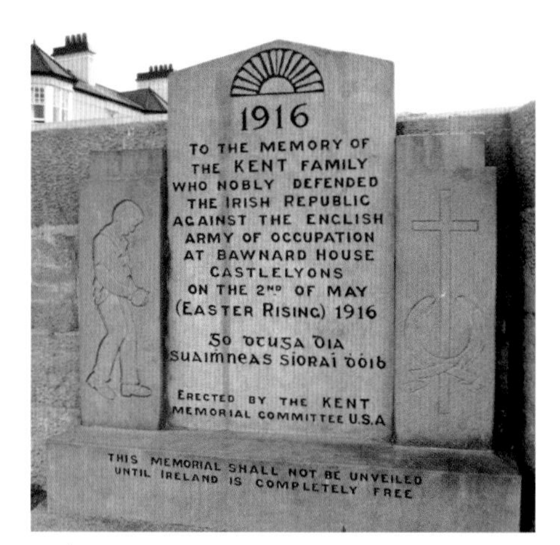

*Clockwise, top left: Éamonn Ceannt, Michael Mallin, Seán Heuston and Con Colbert, were executed on Monday, 8th May. Ceannt had resolutely led operations at the SDU. According to Wylie, he was the most dignified of any of the accused at the trials. Mallin, a former NCO in the British Army, with Indian service, led the main ICA detachment in St Stephen's Green and the College of Surgeons. Con Colbert, a charismatic young man, Chief Scout in Fianna Éireann, had commanded the Marrowbone Lane garrison. Seán Heuston, also of Fianna Éireann, had held out for three days at the Mendicity Institution, under fierce assault.*

*Below near left: Thomas Kent, overlooked in the 1916 story. As part of a countrywide roundup, on 2nd May, a party of RIC arrived after daybreak at the Kent farmhouse in Co. Cork to arrest Thomas and his brother David, prominent republicans. As Head Constable Rowe knocked on the door and demanded that everyone come out, shots rang out, killing Rowe. A gun battle ensued. David was badly wounded. Another brother was mortally wounded. Thomas and another brother, William, were arrested. Far left: memorial at Fermoy.*

*Right: the Kent family farmhouse at Castlelyons, Co. Cork.*

*Middle right: Thomas (the postcard inaccurately refers to 'Edmund') on left, and William Kent, under arrest. Both were court-martialled at Cork Detention Barracks on 4th May. Thomas was sentenced to death and shot on 9th May.*

*Unionist Ireland's then house-journal, 'The Irish Times' in its first post-Rising edition (1st May) stated that the "surgeon's knife has been put to the corruption of the body of Ireland, and its course must not be stayed until the whole malignant growth has been removed".*

*Official nationalist Ireland was ambivalent; the handbill, below near right, condemns the response to the executions made by Redmond in the House of Commons.*

*Two days before James Connolly's execution, William Martin Murphy's 'Irish Independent' displayed no ambivalence about punishment of Murphy's bête noire. The 10th May issue urged in an editorial, far right, that "the worst of the ringleaders be singled out and dealt with as they deserve". Just in case the point was missed, the same edition helpfully included a photograph of Connolly.*

Irish Rebellion, May, 1916.

Arrest of Edmund Kent, at 4 a.m. He was subsequently shot.

**JOHN REDMOND and the EXECUTIONS.**

On the evening of the 3rd May, 1916, after the British Premier had announced—amid the cheers of the English Whigs and Tories and the Redmondites—that **Pearse, MacDonagh** and **Clarke** had been shot that morning, and while **Joseph Plunkett, Edward Daly, Cornelius Colbert** and **Michael O'Hanrahan** were lying in the condemned cell, John Redmond rose in the British House of Commons and said:—

> **"This outbreak happily seems to be over. It has been dealt with with firmness which was not only right, but it was the duty of the Government to so deal with it . . . I do beg the Government not to show undue harshness or severity to the great masses of those who are implicated, on whose shoulders lies a guilt far different from that which lies upon the INSTIGATORS and PROMOTERS of this outbreak."**

Redmond thus signified his approval of the Execution of the Leaders.

Redmond uttered this speech at 4 p.m. in the British House of Commons on May 3rd. Eleven hours later, Plunkett, Daly, O'Hanrahan and Colbert were shot by the British Government's orders.

***Who will vote for the nominee of Redmond, the approver and inciter of the execution of Joseph Plunkett?***

Printed by O'Loughlin, Murphy & Boland, Ltd., Dublin, and published by J. B. Goff, Solicitor, Boyle, Election Agent for Count Plunkett.

might be dealt with leniently; also those who came out under a misconception. When, however, we come to some of the ringleaders, instigators, and fomentors not yet dealt with, we must make an exception. If these men are treated with too great leniency they will take it as an indication of weakness on the part of the Government, and the consequences may not be satisfactory. They may be more truculent than ever, and it is therefore, necessary that society should be protected against their activity. Some of these leaders are more guilty and played a more sinister part in the campaign than those who have been already punished with severity and it would hardly be fair to treat these leniently because the cry for clemency has been raised while those no more guilty than they have been severely punished. Weakness to such men at this stage may be fatal. A little firmness displayed some months ago would have saved much but it would be a mistake to be too firm and too severe when all the harm has been done. Let the worst of the ringleaders be singled out and dealt with as they deserve; but we hope there will be no holocaust or slaughter and no consigning of hundreds of irresponsible and misguided

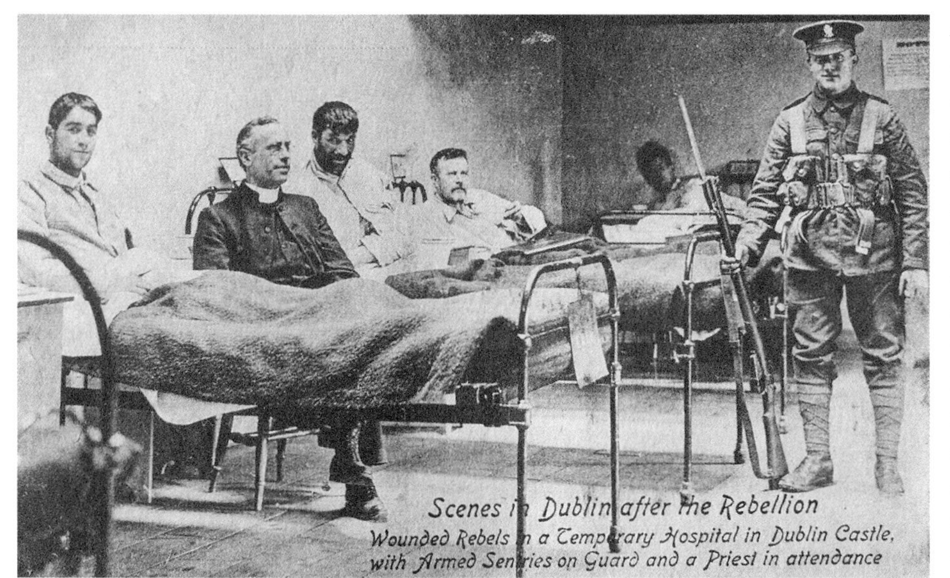


*As WW I ground on, Dublin Port began to receive hospital ships on a monthly basis carrying wounded soldiers from the front lines. As local hospital resources were overstretched, a Red Cross hospital had been set up in Dublin Castle. On the outbreak of the Rising, it was used to treat military and civilian wounded. Some rooms were pressed into service to house wounded republicans, seen under guard of a soldier with a fixed bayonet, in this postcard, left.*

*Connolly had been severely wounded on Thursday; a shin bone was shattered, above his left ankle. After the surrender on Saturday, he was carried by Volunteers on a stretcher through the streets to Dublin Castle, accompanied by British soldiers. Under heavy guard, he was placed in a bed, (reputedly in this room, left, which had previously been reserved for royalty) and his wound was dressed.*

*James Connolly, far left, and Seán MacDermott, near left, were executed on 12th May. MacDermott, despite being afflicted by polio in 1911, was the most dynamic of all. Together with Clarke, he had revitalised the IRB. One historian called him the 'mainspring' of the planning and implementation of the Rising.*

*Despite Wylie's objections that Connolly was wounded, Maxwell insisted that the Court be convened in hospital. On 9th May the Court Martial proceeded there (without Wylie as prosecutor, who only heard about it afterwards). Connolly was propped up in his bed, with three judges presiding. The prisoner was found guilty, and Maxwell confirmed the death sentence the same day.*

*Right: Lillie Connolly. At midnight on 11th May, she was brought to see her husband. As she realised that the end was imminent, Connolly requested: "Don't cry, Lillie, you'll unman me". As she spoke about his beautiful life, he added "hasn't it been a full life and isn't this a good end?"*

*Connolly was put on a stretcher in a horse-drawn ambulance which raced at speed to Kilmainham. As dawn broke, he was delivered, blindfolded, through the gate, middle right, directly to the gaol yard. He was placed on a kitchen chair (rough sketch, near right, by the presiding British officer), and shot at the point now marked by a cross.*

*Connolly's ghastly form of execution caused particular public outrage. Far right: his death colourfully depicted in this New York poster of October 1916.*

SCHEDULE.

Date 4th May. 1916. NO.

| Name of Alleged Offender (a) | Offence charged | Plea | Finding, and if convicted, Sentence (b) | How dealt with by Confirming Officer |
|---|---|---|---|---|
| Constance Georgina Markievicz. | 1. Did an act to wit did take part in an armed rebellion and in the waging of war against His Majesty the King, such act being of such a nature as to calculated to be prejudical to the Defence of the Realm and being done with the intention and for the purpose of assisting the enemy. | Not Guilty. | Guilty. Death by being shot. The Court recommend the prisoner to mercy solely and only on account of her sex. | Confirmed. But I commute the sentence to one of Penal Servitude for life. |
| Alternative. | 2. Did attempt to cause disaffection among the civilian population of His Majesty. | Guilty. | | |

(a) If the name of the person charged is unknown, he may be described as unknown with such addition as will identify him.

(b) Recommendation to mercy to be inserted in this column.

J.G. Maxwell
Convening Officer.

C.J. Blackader, Brig-Gen.
President.

Promulgated this 6th day of May 1916.
Kilmainham Goal, Dublin.

H. Anderson, Capt.

*Countess Markievicz (far left, escorted by a wardress) was sentenced to death on 4th May, with a recommendation that mercy be shown 'solely and only on account of her sex'. Maxwell, having been instructed by Asquith that there should be no female executions, commuted the sentence to penal servitude for life. Wylie, the prosecutor, later controversially claimed that she had said at her trial "you can't shoot a woman". There is no mention of this in the Court records (schedule, near left) which recorded that she said "I went out to fight for Ireland's freedom and it doesn't matter what happens to me".*

*Left: Eamon de Valera was lucky: his death sentence was commuted by Maxwell. All the other Dublin commandants had been executed. De Valera had been incarcerated at first in Pembroke town hall in Ballsbridge and had missed the initial screening and the first wave of executions. Maxwell, in a meeting with Wylie, showed him a telegram from Asquith pressing for curtailment of executions, and asked who was next. "De Valera", replied Wylie, and assured Maxwell, who hadn't heard of him, that he was not important and was unlikely to make trouble in future. His American background was not discussed at this meeting.*

*On 12th May, Asquith made an impromptu visit to Ireland, arriving scarcely after the last volleys had rung out in Kilmainham. He visited the prisoners in Richmond Barracks, right, and promised them 'the best food possible'. Later, the soldiers on guard reportedly begged food from the prisoners. Asquith was received with warmth when walking about Dublin. Demonstrating a lamentable naivety, he concluded that a better future would result from more frequent royal visits.*

*A roundup of 'Sinn Féiners' was made across the country. Thousands were interned in a wide range of British prisons. Many were eventually transferred to Frongoch camp (sketches by prisoners, right) in North Wales, previously a camp for German prisoners of war.*

*The places where the Irish prisoners were interned proved to be training grounds for the next phase of the independence struggle. Michael Collins (arrow) is seen amongst the prisoners at Stafford Gaol, right.*

*Overleaf: 'High Treason' by Sir John Lavery. This large canvas depicts Roger Casement's appeal on 17th July 1916 against his sentence of death for treason, at his trial in June. The appeal was dismissed.*

*The trial for treason of Sir Roger Casement, left, has been described as an elaborate show trial, which, when added to an incompetent defence (no senior British barrister could be found) meant the result was predetermined. The prosecuting council, the Attorney General, Sir FE Smith, had some knowledge of treason against the Crown, having been a prominent supporter of the UVF's armed defiance of the Home Rule Bill, passed by Parliament.*

*Casement was found guilty on 29th June. Below left: the court record that includes the sentence – "Your crime was that of assisting the King's enemies, that is the Empire of Germany, during the terrible war in which we are engaged... that you be taken...to a place of execution...and that you be there hanged by the neck until...dead."*

*Below: one of the exhibits at the trial: a cypher sheet, found after Casement dropped it near McKenna's Fort.*

226

scrap of paper that might or might not be redeemed, I felt over there in America, that my first duty was to keep Irishmen at home in the only army that could safeguard our national existence. If small nationalities were to be the pawns in this game of embattled giants, I saw no reason why Ireland should shed her blood in any cause but her own, and if that be treason beyond the seas I am not ashamed to avow it or to answer for it here with my life. And when we had the doctrine of Unionist loyalty at last—"Mausers and Kaisers and any king you like," and I have heard that at Hamburg, not far from Limburg on the Lahn—I felt I needed no other warrant than that these words conveyed—to go forth and do likewise. The difference between us was that the Unionist champions chose a path they felt would lead to the woolsack; while I went a road I knew must lead to the dock. And the event proves we were both right. The difference between us was that my "treason" was based on a ruthless sincerity that forced me to attempt in time and season to carry out in action what I said in word—whereas their treason lay in verbal incitements that they knew need never be made good in their bodies. And so, I am prouder to stand here to-day in the traitor's dock to answer this impeachment than to fill the place of my right honourable accusers.

We have been told, we have been asked to hope, that after this war Ireland will get Home Rule—as a reward for the life blood shed in a cause that whoever else its success may benefit, can surely not benefit Ireland. And what will Home Rule be in return for what its vague promise has taken and still hopes to take away from Ireland? It is not necessary to climb the painful stairs of Irish history—that treadmill of a nation whose labours are as vain for her own uplifting as the convict's exertions are for his redemption—to review the long list of British promises made only to be broken—of Irish hopes raised only to be dashed to the ground. Home Rule when it comes, if come it does, will find an Ireland drained of all that is vital to its very existence—unless it be that unquenchable hope we build on the graves of the dead. We are told that if Irishmen go by the thousand to die, not for Ireland, but for Flanders, for Belgium—for a patch of sand on the deserts of Mesopotamia, or a rocky trench on the heights of Gallipoli, they are winning self-government for Ireland. But if they dare to lay down their lives on their native soil, if they dare to dream even that freedom can be won only at home by men resolved to fight for it there, then they are traitors to their country, and their dream and their deaths alike are phases of a dishonourable phantasy. But history is not so recorded in other lands. In Ireland alone in this 20th century, is loyalty held to be a crime. If loyalty be something less than love and more than law then we have had enough of such loyality for Ireland or Irishmen. If we are to be indicted as criminals—to be shot as murderers, to be imprisoned as convicts, because our offence is that we love Ireland more than we value our lives, then I know not what virtue resides in any offer of self-government held out to brave men on such terms. Self-government is our right, a thing born in us at birth; a thing no more to be doled out to us or withheld from us by another people, than the right to life itself—than the right to feel the sun or smell the flowers—or to love our kind. It is only from the convict these things are withheld for crime committed and proven—and Ireland that has wronged no man, that has injured no land, that has sought no dominion over others—Ireland is treated to-day among the nations of the world as if she was a convicted criminal. If it be treason to fight against ~~such an~~ unnatural fate as this, then I am proud to be a rebel—and shall cling to my "rebellion" with the last drop of my blood. If there be no right of rebellion against a state of things that no savage tribe would endure without resistance, than am I sure that it is better for men to fight and die without right than to live in such a state of right as this. Where all your

227

Fourth Day.
29 June 1916.

rights become only an accumulated wrong; where men must beg with bated breath for leave to subsist in their own land, to think their own thoughts, to sing their own songs, to garner the fruit of their own labours—and even while they beg, to see these things inexorably withdrawn from them—then surely it is a braver, a saner, and a truer thing to be a rebel in act and deed against such circumstances as these, than tamely to accept it as the natural lot of men.

My Lord, I have done. Gentlemen of the jury, I wish to thank you for your verdict. I hope you will not take amiss what I said, or think that I made any imputation upon your truthfulness or your integrity when I spoke and said that this was not a trial by my peers. I maintain that I have a natural right to be tried in that natural jurisdiction, Ireland, my own country, and I would put it to you, how would you feel in the converse case, or rather how would all men here feel in the converse case if an Englishman had landed here in England and the Crown or the Government for its own purposes had conveyed him secretly from England to Ireland under a false name, committed him to prison under a false name, and brought him before a tribunal in Ireland under a statute which they knew involved a trial before an Irish jury? How would you feel yourselves, as Englishmen if that man was to be submitted to trial by a jury in a land inflamed against him and believing him to be a criminal, when his only crime was that he had cared for England more than for Ireland.

The USHER: Oyez. My Lords, the King's Justices, do strictly charge and command all manner of persons to keep silence whilst sentence of death is passing upon the prisoner at the Bar, upon pain of imprisonment.

The LORD CHIEF JUSTICE: Sir Roger David Casement, you have been found guilty of treason, the gravest crime known to the law, and upon evidence which in our opinion is conclusive of guilt. Your crime was that of assisting the King's enemies, that is the Empire of Germany, during the terrible war in which we are engaged. The duty now devolves upon me of passing sentence upon you, and it is that you be taken hence to a lawful prison, and thence to a place of execution, and that you be there hanged by the neck until you be dead. And the Sheriffs of the Counties of London and Middlesex are and each of them is hereby charged with the execution of this Judgment, and may the Lord have mercy on your soul.

Mr. JUSTICE AVERY: Amen.

Mr. ARTEMUS JONES: My Lord, there are two cousins here of Sir Roger Casement who desire to see him for a few minutes to bid him good-bye.

The LORD CHIEF JUSTICE: There is no provision made for an interview here; application must be made in the ordinary course elsewhere.

Mr. ARTEMUS JONES: If your Lordship pleases.

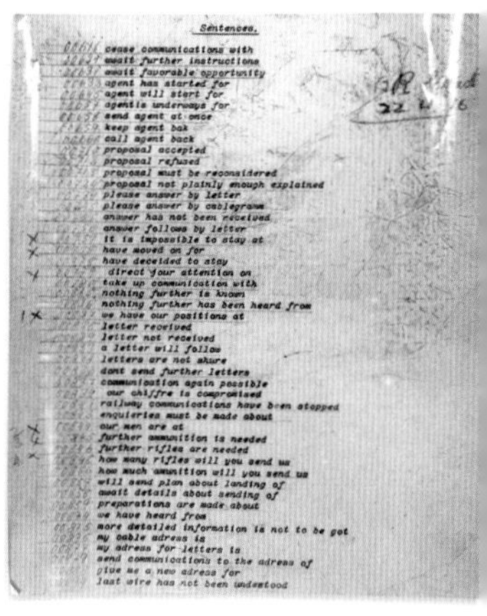

Sentences.

cease communications with
await further instructions
await favorable opportunity
agent has started for
agent will start for
agent is underways for
send agent at once
keep agent bak
call agent back
proposal accepted
proposal refused
proposal must be reconsidered
proposal not plainly enough explained
please answer by letter
please answer by cablegramm
answer has not been received
answer follows by letter
it is impossible to stay at
have moved on for
have deceided to stay
direct your attention on
take up communication with
nothing further is known
nothing further has been heard from
we have our positions at
letter received
letter not received
a letter will follow
letters are not shure
dont send further letters
communication again possible
our chiffre is compromised
railway communications have been stopped
enquieries must be made about
our men are at
further ammunition is needed
further rifles are needed
how many rifles will you send us
how much amunition will you send us
will send plan about landing of
await details about sending of
preparations are made about
we have heard from
more detailed information is not to be got
my cable adress is
my adress for letters is
send communications to the adress of
give me a new adress for
last wire has not been understood

*Casement was smeared by the organised leaking, to opinion formers, of extracts from diaries found at his previous London lodgings, which detailed homosexual activities.*

*Piling on indignity: Casement received this document, near right, in Pentonville Gaol on 11th July informing him that he had been stripped of his knighthood. The annotations and heavily crossed-out additions attest to the emotions that it generated. Casement had embraced Catholicism in his last days. Far right: a Catholic Truth Society pamphlet, (given by a friend) for 'the sorrowful and suffering'. He marked many comforting passages within, and on one page he wrote "2nd August 1916...my last day". He was hanged in Pentonville on the 3rd. Above, far right: Casement's last writings: "... and if I die tomorrow bury me in Ireland"; "I hope that God will be with me to the end and that all my faults and failures will be blotted out..."*

*Initially Casement's wish to be buried in Ireland was not to be. He was buried in Pentonville. However, in 1965, in a 'glasnost' moment, Harold Wilson allowed Casement's remains to be repatriated. He was buried at Glasnevin, right, and President de Valera, then aged 82, gave the oration.*

Copy

Seal.

(Signed) GEORGE R.I.

GEORGE THE FIFTH, by the Grace of God of the United Kingdom of Great Britain and Ireland and of the British Dominions beyond the Seas King, Defender of the Faith, Emperor of India, Sovereign and Chief of the Most Distinguished Order of Saint Michael and Saint George; to all to whom these Presents shall come, Greeting.

WHEREAS by the Twenty-sixth Clause of the Statutes of Our said Most Distinguished Order bearing date the Tenth day of October, One Thousand Nine Hundred and Eleven it is (amongst other things) Ordained that if any Companion of the said Most Distinguished Order be convicted of Treason, Cowardice, Felony or of any Grave Misdemeanour derogatory to his honour as a gentleman, he shall forthwith be Degraded from the said Most Distinguished Order by an Ordinance signed by the Sovereign and Sealed with the Seal of the said Most Distinguished Order, and thereupon his name in the Register shall be erased.

AND WHEREAS it has been represented to Us that Sir Roger Casement, Knight, a Companion of the Most Distinguished Order

ORDINANCE

degrading and removing

SIR ROGER CASEMENT, KNIGHT, C.M.G.,

from the Most Distinguished

ORDER of SAINT MICHAEL and SAINT GEORGE.

Rood and Staff.

For the Sorrowful and Suffering.

"Virga tua, et baculus tuus, ipsa me consolata sunt."
—Psl. xxii., 4.

"Thy rood and thy staff; they have comforted me."

DUBLIN:
CATHOLIC TRUTH SOCIETY OF IRELAND,
24 Upper O'Connell Street.

PRICE 5 CENTS

THE Fatherland

(TITLE REG. U.S. PAT. OFF.)

A Weekly

Vol. IV

MAY 17th, 1916

No. 15



Drawn for THE FATHERLAND by A. Staehle

MORGAN'S GREAT WAR PARADE, MAY 13, 1916

By Charles A. Collman

THE FATHERLAND BELIEVES IN PREPAREDNESS FOR THE BENEFIT OF DEMOCRACY, NOT FOR THE BENEFIT OF WALL STREET

*Nervousness about the loyalty of Irish regiments in the British Army meant a positive spin was strongly promoted. Above: the 'Illustrated London News' depicts Irish troops charging enemy trenches, "saying what they think of treason at home".*
*Left: in May 1916 this German-American weekly depicted a heroic Pearse greeting George Washington, with the message: "We fought the same foe & for the same reason". The British were nervous about American reaction to the Rising and its impact on possible US entry to WW I. As it turned out, Irish America was not all-powerful; President Wilson was essentially anglophile and German ineptness (resumption of unrestricted submarine warfare and anti-US plotting in Mexico) led to a declaration of war by the USA on Germany in early 1917.*

*Near right: headlined "Germany's futile attempt to pervert Irish Troops", a British magazine shows a placard placed opposite the Royal Munster Fusiliers' trenches: "English guns are firing on your wifes (sic) and children!"*
*A 'Royal Commission on the Rebellion in Ireland' began hearings on 18th May. Tolerance of militias and poor intelligence were among its conclusions, also that the Irish system of government was dysfunctional. Far right: Sir Matthew Nathan, Under-Secretary, and Augustine Birrell, Chief Secretary, leaving the enquiry, having resigned in early May.*
*In mid-1917, the prisoners were unconditionally released. Right: rapturous welcome at Westland Row. It was in stark contrast to the abuse many had sufferred as they trudged to the cattle boats on the quays a year before.*

*Above: the most obscure and secret location possible was chosen to bury the executed 'ringleaders'. The bodies were interred without coffins in quicklime. They were placed in a pit dug at the rear of a yard at Arbour Hill Detention Barracks in Dublin.*

*Left: mythical, heroic: a poster depicts the Birth of the Irish Republic in 1916.*

*In the aftermath of the executions, public opinion began to swing in favour of the insurgents. By 1919, the First Dáil, elected by public suffrage, endorsed the declaration of a Republic. The War of Independence led to the Truce and the Treaty. The Civil War that followed in 1922 tried the mettle of the 26-county Free State. The tension between the ideals of 1916 and actuality has created difficulties for Irish political leaders over the decades.*

*Above: in serried ranks: British casualties of the Rising repose at the well-maintained but little-visited Grangegorman military cemetery, Blackhorse Avenue, in Dublin.*
*The Garden of Remembrance was built in the 1960s, with a somewhat Soviet-style statue, right, as its centrepiece. It is dedicated to the memory of "all those who gave their lives in the cause of Irish Freedom" and covers uprisings from 1798 to 1921.*
*Below right: 1916 memorial at Glasnevin cemetery.*
*Below: 'His Easter Offering'. This poster portrays the sacrifice of 1916 as a form of secular sanctification: the heavenly angel; the figure of Ireland with tricolour; the fallen Volunteer.*

*Above: mosaic at the Garden of Remembrance – in Celtic myth, to signify the end of a battle, weapons were broken and thrown into a river or lake.*
*The executed leaders are buried at Arbour Hill, now a central place of commemoration. Reflecting the clarity of the uplifting Proclamation, its words are chiselled in clear detail on the boundary wall, left.*
*In 1966, 'Our Boys' presented the Rising as glorious and inspirational, left. In its modest way, the image captures the essence of its legacy. The Rising was indeed a small affair that was militarily suppressed. However, its strength lay in its dramatic symbolism; after centuries of failed revolutions, it allowed the Irish people to see what was possible – that the strong British grasp established over Ireland could indeed be broken. Connolly wrote, as the flames rose around Sackville Street, and the physical battle was patently lost: "Courage Boys, we are winning." He was right, as the week's events were to later reverberate in Ireland and around other parts of the world.*

# Appendix 1

IRISH WAR NEWS

THE IRISH REPUBLIC.

"IF THE GERMANS CONQUERED ENGLAND."

*The following article appeared as the lead in 'Irish War News' published, by the republican forces on Tuesday April 25th 1916 (most likely it had been pre-prepared for a periodical of the republican mosquito press 'Honesty'). The article is surprisingly sophisticated for a news-sheet that was distributed from the revolutionary barricades. The writer has taken a recent article in the 'New Statesman' and, with delicious irony, uses it to present as good a case for Irish independence and the underlying rationale for the Rising, as has been written.*

### "IF THE GERMANS CONQUERED ENGLAND"

In the London *New Statesman* for April 1st, an article is published – "If the Germans Conquered England," which has the appearance of a very clever piece of satire written by an Irishman. The writer draws a picture of England under German rule, almost every detail of which exactly fits the case of Ireland at the present day. Some of the sentences are so exquisitely appropriate that it is impossible to believe that the writer had not Ireland in his mind when he wrote them. For instance:–

*"England would be constantly irritated by the lofty moral utterances of German statesmen who would assert – quite sincerely, no doubt – that England was free, freer indeed than she had ever been before. Prussian freedom, they would explain, was the only real freedom, and therefore England was free. They would point to the flourishing railways and farms and colleges. They would possibly point to the contingent of M.P.'s, which was permitted, in spite of its deplorable disorderliness, to sit in a permanent minority in the Reichstag. And not only would the Englishman have to listen to a constant flow of speeches of this sort; he would find a respectable official Press secret(ary) brought over by the Government to say the same things over and over, every day of the week. He would find too, that his children were coming home from school with new ideas of history… They would ask him if it was true that until the Germans came England had been an unruly country, constantly engaged in civil war… The object of every schoolbook would be to make the English child grow up in the notion that the history of his country was a thing to forget, and that the one bright spot in it was the fact that it had been conquered by cultured Germany."*

*"If there was a revolt, German statesmen would deliver grave speeches about "disloyalty," "ingratitude," "reckless agitators who would ruin their country's prosperity… Prussian soldiers would be encamped in every barracks – the English conscripts having been sent out of the country to be trained in Germany, or to fight the Chinese – in order to come to the aid of German morality, should English sedition come to blows with it."*

*"England would be exhorted to abandon her own genius in order to imitate the genius of her conquerors, to forget her own history for a larger history, to give up her language for a "universal" language – in other words, to destroy her household gods one by one, and put in their place alien gods. Such an England would be an England without a soul, without even a mind. She would be a nation of slaves, even though every slave in the country had a chicken in his pot and a golden dish to serve it on."*

Put "Ireland" in the place of "England" in these extracts and "England" in the place of "Germany," and it will be admitted that the humiliating state of national subjection in which we live, and the cunning methods of spiritual conquest practised on us by England have seldom been better described. If the article was not written by an Irishman in a bitterly satiric mood, it shows how well Englishmen understand how the treatment they have been accustomed to apply to other nations would feel, applied to themselves. But my own opinion certainly is, that every sentence I have quoted stamps the article as the production of a very able Sinn Féiner.

# Appendix 2

*The 1916 Proclamation is clear, precise and inspirational. The original poster is difficult to read, given the exigencies of the time (two years into the Great War) and in particular the poor-quality paper, the shortage of type – especially for the largest letters – and the limitations of the printing press that was used . The text is reproduced here.*

**POBLACHT NA H EIREANN**

**THE PROVISIONAL GOVERNMENT<br>OF THE IRISH REPUBLIC<br>TO THE PEOPLE OF IRELAND**

IRISHMEN AND IRISHWOMEN: In the name of God and of the dead generations from which she receives her old tradition of nationhood, Ireland, through us, summons her children to her flag and strikes for her freedom.

Having organised and trained her manhood through her secret revolutionary organisation, the Irish Republican Brotherhood, and through her open military organisations, the Irish Volunteers and the Irish Citizen Army, having patiently perfected her discipline, having resolutely waited for the right moment to reveal itself, she now seizes that moment, and, supported by her exiled children in America and by gallant allies in Europe, but relying in the first on her own strength, she strikes in full confidence of victory.

We declare the right of the people of Ireland to the ownership of Ireland, and to the unfettered control of Irish destinies, to be sovereign and indefeasible. The long usurpation of that right by a foreign people and government has not extinguished the right, nor can it ever be extinguished except by the destruction of the Irish people. In every generation the Irish people have asserted their right to national freedom and sovereignty; six times during the last three hundred years they have asserted it to arms. Standing on that fundamental right and again asserting it in arms in the face of the world, we hereby proclaim the Irish Republic as a Sovereign Independent State, and we pledge our lives and the lives of our comrades-in-arms to the cause of its freedom, of its welfare, and of its exaltation among the nations.

The Irish Republic is entitled to, and hereby claims, the allegiance of every Irishman and Irishwoman. The Republic guarantees religious and civil liberty, equal rights and equal opportunities to all its citizens, and declares its resolve to pursue the happiness and prosperity of the whole nation and of all its parts, cherishing all of the children of the nation equally, and oblivious of the differences carefully fostered by an alien government, which have divided a minority from the majority in the past.

Until our arms have brought the opportune moment for the establishment of a permanent National Government, representative of the whole people of Ireland and elected by the suffrages of all her men and women, the Provisional Government, hereby constituted, will administer the civil and military affairs of the Republic in trust for the people.

We place the cause of the Irish Republic under the protection of the Most High God, Whose blessing we invoke upon our arms, and we pray that no one who serves that cause will dishonour it by cowardice, inhumanity, or rapine. In this supreme hour the Irish nation must, by its valour and discipline and by the readiness of its children to sacrifice themselves for the common good, prove itself worthy of the august destiny to which it is called.

**Signed on Behalf of the Provisional Government,**

**THOMAS J. CLARKE**

**SEAN Mac DIARMADA, THOMAS MacDONAGH**

**P. H. PEARSE, EAMONN CEANNT**

**JAMES CONNOLLY. JOSEPH PLUNKETT.**

# Bibliography

***Principal Libraries, Museums & Archives consulted:***
Allen Library, Dublin; American Irish Historical Society, New York; Capuchin Archives, Dublin; Central Catholic Library, Dublin; Dublin City Library & Archive; Glasnevin Cemetery Museum, Dublin; Guinness Archives, Dublin; Irish Architectural Archive, Dublin; Irish Labour History Museum and Archive, Dublin; Irish Railway Records Society, Dublin; Military Archives (Military Service Pensions Collection, Bureau of Military History Witness Statements), Dublin; Military Museum, The Curragh; National Library of Ireland, Dublin; National Archives, Dublin; National Maritime Museum, Dún Laoghaire; National Museum of Ireland, Dublin; New York Public Library; South Dublin Libraries, Tallaght.

***Periodicals:***
General Irish and British newspapers
History Ireland
Irish Historical Studies
Journal of the Irish Railway Record Society
The Defence Forces Magazine: An Cosantóir
The Irish Sword
University Review

***Books on Easter 1916 recommended in the first instance:***
Caulfield, M., *The Easter Rebellion,* Gill & Macmillan, Dublin, 1995.
Foy, M., Barton, B., *The Easter Rising*, History Press, Stroud, 2011.
O'Brien P., *Battleground, the Battle for the General Post Office, 1916,* New Island, Dublin, 2015.
O'Brien P., *Blood on the Streets, 1916 & the Battle for Mount Street Bridge*, Mercier Press, Cork, 2008.
O'Brien P., *Uncommon Valour, 1916 & the Battle for the South Dublin Union*, New Island, Dublin, 2010.
O'Brien P., *Field of Fire, the Battle of Ashbourne, 1916*, New Island, Dublin, 2012.
O'Brien P., *Shootout, the Battle for St Stephen's Green, 1916*, New Island, Dublin, 2013.
Townshend, C., *Easter 1916, The Irish Rebellion*, Penguin Books, London, 2006.

***Books:***
*(No date: ND; No publisher information: NP; No author information: NA)*
(NA) *Cuimhneachán 1916*, National Gallery of Ireland, Dublin, 1966.
(NA) *Dublin after the Six Days' Insurrection*, Mecredy, Percy & Co., Dublin 1916.
(NA) *Sinn Fein Rebellion Handbook*, Irish Times, Dublin, 1916.
(NA) *The 'Sinn Féin' Revolt Illustrated*, Helys Ltd., Dublin 1916.
(NA) *The Irish Rebellion, The 2/6th Sherwood Foresters' part in the Defeat of the Rebels in 1916*, Sherwood Foresters, Chesterfield, 1961.
(NA) *The Rebellion in Dublin, April 1916*, Eason & Son, Dublin, 1916.
Andrews, C., *Dublin Made Me*, Lilliput Press, Dublin, 2001.
Arthur, G., *General Sir John Maxwell*, John Murray, London, 1932.
Balfour, G., *The armoured train, its development and usage,* Batsford, London, 1981.
Barry, M., *The Green Divide, an Illustrated History of the Irish Civil War*, Andalus Press, Dublin, 2014.
Barton, B., *From Behind a Closed Door*, Blackstaff Press, Belfast, 2002.
Bateson, R., *Dead and Buried in Dublin*, Irish Graves Publications, Dublin, 2002.
Bateson, R., *Memorials of the Easter Rising*, Irish Graves Publications, Dublin, 2013.
Bateson, R., *The rising dead : RIC & DMP,* Irish Graves Publications, Dublin 2012.
Bateson, R., *They died by Pearse's side,* Irish Graves Publications, Dublin, 2010.
Béaslaí, P., *Michael Collins and the Making of a New Ireland*, Phoenix Publishing Company, Dublin, 1926.
Beckett, I., *The Army and the Curragh Incident 1914*, Bodley Head, London, 1986.
Beckett, J. C., *The Making of Modern Ireland 1603-1923*, Faber & Faber, London, 1972.
Bowyer Bell, J., *The Secret Army: the IRA 1916-1979*, Poolbeg, Dublin, 1990.
Brennan-Whitmore, W., *Dublin Burning*, Gill & Macmillan, Dublin, 1996.
Brunicardi, D., *The Seahound*, Collins Press, Cork, 2001.
Casey, C., *The Buildings of Ireland: Dublin*, Yale University Press, New Haven and London, 2005.
Chambers, C., *Ireland in the Newsreels*, Irish Academic Press, Dublin, 2012.
Clayton, X., *Aud*, GAC, Plymouth, 2007.
Coakley, D., O'Doherty, M., ed., *Borderlands*, Royal College of Surgeons, Dublin, 2002.
Collins, L., *James Connolly*, O'Brien Press, Dublin, 2012.
Connell, J., *Dublin in Rebellion: A Directory 1913-1923*, Lilliput Press, Dublin, 2009.
Connell, J., *Dublin Rising 1916*, Wordwell, Dublin, 2015
Connolly, C., *Michael Collins*, Weidenfeld & Nicholson, London, 1996.

Coogan, T. P., *1916: The Easter Rising*, Orion Books, London, 2005.
Coogan, T. P., *De Valera: Long Fellow, Long Shadow*, Hutchinson, London, 1993.
Coogan, T. P., *Michael Collins*, Arrow Books, London, 1990.
Cooke, P., *A History of Kilmainham Gaol*, Brunswick Press, Dublin, 2005.
Crowe, C., ed., *Guide to the Military Service (1916-1923) Pensions Collection*, Óglaigh na hÉireann, Dublin, 2012.
Crowley, B., *Patrick Pearse, a Life in Pictures*, Mercier Press, Cork, 2013.
De Courcy Ireland, J., *The Sea and the Easter Rising 1916*, Maritime Institute of Ireland, Dún Laoghaire, 1966.
De Rosa, P., *Rebels, the Irish Rising of 1916*, Bantam Press, London, 1990.
Devoy, J., *Recollections of an Irish Rebel*, Irish University Press, Shannon, 1969.
Dorney, J., *Peace after the Final Battle, the Story of the Irish Revolution, 1912-1924*, New Island, Dublin, 2014.
Dorney, J., *The Story of the Easter Rising*, Green Lamp Editions, Dublin, 2010.
Dudley Edwards, O., Pyle, F., *1916, the Easter Rising*, Macgibbon & Kee, London, 1968.
Dudley Edwards, R., *Patrick Pearse, the Triumph of Failure,* Gollancz, London, 1977.
Dwayne, D., *Life of Eamon De Valera Illustrated*, Talbot Press, Dublin, 1927.
Fallon, L., *Dublin Fire Brigade and the Irish Revolution*, South Dublin Libraries, Dublin, 2012.
Fanning, R., *Fatal Path: British Government and Irish Revolution*, Faber & Faber, London, 2013.
Feeney, B., *Sean MacDiarmada*, O'Brien Press, Dublin, 2014.
Ferguson, S., *GPO Staff in 1916*, Mercier Press, Cork, 2012.
Ferriter, D., *A Nation and not a Rabble, the Irish Revolution 1913-23*, Profile Books, London, 2015.
Fitzgerald, D., *Desmond's Rising*, Liberties Press, Dublin, 1968.
Fletcher Vane, F., *Agin the Governments*, Sampson Low, Marston & Co., London, 1929.
Fox, R., *The History of the Irish Citizen Army*, James Connolly Debating Society, Belfast, 2013.
Gallagher, M., *Éamonn Ceannt*, O'Brien Press, Dublin, 2014.
Garden, S., *The Alderman, Alderman Tom Kelly and Dublin Corporation*, Dublin City Library and Archive, Dublin, 2007.
Gibney, J., *Seán Heuston*, , O'Brien Press, Dublin, 2013.
Gillis, L., *Revolution in Dublin: A Photographic History 1913-1923*, Mercier Press, Cork, 2013.
Gillis, L., *Women of the Irish Revolution*, Mercier Press, Cork, 2014.
Golway, T., *Irish Rebel, John Devoy and America's Fight for Irish Freedom*, St Martin's Press, New York, 1998.
Good, J., *Enchanted by Dreams*, Brandon, Dingle, 1996.
Greaves, D., *Liam Mellows and the Irish Revolution*, Lawrence & Wishart, London, 1971.
Greaves, D., *The Life and Times of James Connolly*, Lawrence & Wishart, London, 1986.
Griffith, K., O'Grady, T., *Curious Journey*, Hutchinson, London, 1982.
Gwynn, D., *The History of Partition (1912-1925)*, Browne & Nolan, Dublin, 1950.
Hart, P., *The IRA at War 1916-1923*, Oxford University Press USA, New York, 2005.
Hay, M., *Bulmer Hobson and the Nationalist Movement in 20th-Century Ireland*, Manchester University Press, Manchester, 2009.
Hegarty, S., O'Toole, F., *The Irish Times Book of the 1916 Rising*, Gill & Macmillan, 2006.
Henderson, W. A., *Souvenir Album of the Dublin Fighting*, Brunswick Press, Dublin 1922.
Hodges, R., *Cork and County Cork in the 20th century, contemporary biographies,* Pike & Co., Brighton, 1911.
Hopkinson, M., ed., *Frank Henderson's Easter Rising*, Cork University Press, 1998
Horgan, J., *Sean Lemass, the Enigmatic Patriot*, Gill & Macmillan, Dublin, 1997.
Housley, C., *The Sherwood Foresters in the Easter Rising, Dublin 1916*, Millquest Publications, Nottingham, (ND)
Hughes, B., *Michael Mallin*, O'Brien Press, Dublin, 2012.
Hunt, G., *Blood Upon the Rose, Easter 1916*, O'Brien Press, Dublin, 2012.
Inglis, B., *Roger Casement*, Penguin Books, London, 2002.
Jeffrey, K., *The GPO and the Easter Rising*, Irish Academic Press, Dublin, 2006.
Jenkins, R., *Asquith*, Fontana Books, London, 1967.
Johnson, S., *Johnson's Atlas & Gazetteer of the Railways of Ireland*, Midland Publishing, Leicester, 1997.
Kenna, S., *Thomas MacDonagh*, O'Brien Press, Dublin, 2014.
Kenna, S., *War in the Shadows*, Merrion Press, Kildare, 2014.
Kenny, M., *The Road to Freedom*, National Museum of Ireland, Dublin, 1993.
Keogh, D., *Twentieth-Century Ireland, Revolution and State Building*, Gill & Macmillan, Dublin, 2005.
Kileen, R., *A Short History of the 1916 Rising*, Gill & Macmillan, Dublin, 2009.
Koss, S., *Asquith*, Allen Lane, London, 1976.
Kostick, C., Collins, L., *The Easter Rising, a Guide to Dublin in 1916*, O'Brien Press, Dublin, 2012.
Laffan, M., *Judging WT Cosgrave*, Royal Irish Academy, Dublin, 2014.
Litton, H., *Edward Daly*, O'Brien Press, Dublin, 2013.
Litton, H., *Thomas Clarke*, O'Brien Press, Dublin, 2014.
Lynch, D., *The IRB and the 1916 Insurrection*, Mercier Press, Cork, 1957.
Mac Lochlann, P., *Last Words*, Kilmainham Jail Restoration Society, Dublin, 1971.
Macardle, D., *The Irish Republic*, Merlin Publishing, 1999.
Martin, F. X., ed., *The Howth Gun-Running and the Kilcoole Gun-Running*, Merrion, Dublin, 2014.

Martin, F. X., ed, *The Irish Volunteers 1913-1915*, Merrion, Dublin, 2013.
Matthews, A., *The Irish Citizen Army*, Mercier Press, Cork, 2014.
Matthews, A., *The Kimmage Garrison, 1916*, Four Courts Press, Dublin, 2010.
Maye, B., *Arthur Griffith*, Griffith College Publications, Dublin, 1997.
McCarthy, C., *Cumann na mBan and the Irish Revolution*, Collins Press, Cork, 2007.
McCoole, S., *Easter Widows*, Doubleday Ireland, Dublin, 2014.
McGarry, F., *Rebels: Voices from the Easter Rising*, Penguin Books, 2012.
McGarry, F., *The Rising, Ireland Easter 1916*, Oxford University Press, Oxford, 2010.
McHugh, R., ed., *Dublin 1916*, Arlington Books, London, 1966.
McKenzie, F., *The Irish Rebellion, what happened and why*, C. Arthurs Pearson, London, 1916.
McNally, M., *Easter Rising 1916,* Osprey, Oxford, 2007.
Meakin, G., ed., *Forgotten History, the Kilcoole Gunrunning*, Kilcoole Heritage Group, 2014.
Mitchell, A., *Roger Casement*, O'Brien Press, Dublin, 2013.
Monteith, R., *Casement's Last Adventure*, M. Moynihan, Dublin, 1953.
Morrison, G., *Revolutionary Ireland, a Photographic Record*, Gill & Macmillan, Dublin, 2013.
Mulcahy, R., *My Father the General: Richard Mulcahy and the Military History of the Revolution*, Liberties Press, Dublin, 2009.
Ní Ghairbhí, R., *William Pearse,* O'Brien Press, Dublin, 2015.
Ó Broin, L., *Dublin Castle and the 1916 Rising*, Helicon, Dublin, 1966.
Ó Broin, L., *W. E. Wylie and the Irish Rebellion, 1916-1921*, Gill & Macmillan, Dublin, 1989.
Ó Brolchain, H., *Joseph Plunkett*, O'Brien Press, Dublin, 2012.
Ó Comhraí, C., *Revolution in Connacht, A Photographic History 1913-1923*, Mercier Press, Cork, 2013.
Ó Conchubhair, B., ed., *Dublin's Fighting Story 1916-21*, Mercier Press, Cork. 2009.
Ó Concubhair, P., *The Fenians Were Dreadful Men, the 1867 Rising*, Mercier Press, Cork, 2011.
O'Connor, J., *The Story of the Irish Proclamation*, Anvil Books, Tralee, 1999.
Ó Doibhilin, M., *Anne Devlin*, Kilmainham Tales, Dublin, 2014.
Ó Drisceoil, D., *Peadar O'Donnell*, Cork University Press, Cork, 2001.
Ó Maitiu, S., *W & R Jacob*, Woodfield Press, Dublin, 2001.
Ó Ruairc, P., *Revolution: A Photographic History of Revolutionary Ireland 1913-1923*, Mercier Press, Cork, 2011.
O'Brien P., *A Question of Duty, the Curragh Incident 1914*, New Island, Dublin, 2014.
O'Brien, P., *Arbour Hill Cemetery*, Kilmainham Tales, Dublin, 2012.
O'Brien, P., *Bully's Acre*, Kilmainham Tales, Dublin, 2011.
O'Brien, P., *Royal Hospital Kilmainham*, Kilmainham Tales, Dublin, 2015.
O'Callaghan, J., *Con Colbert*, O'Brien Press, Dublin, 2015.
O'Connor Lysaght, D., *The Communists and the Irish Revolution*, Literéire Publishers, Dublin, 1993.
O'Connor, E., *Reds and the Green*, University College Dublin Press, Dublin, 2004.
O'Donnell, R., ed., *The Impact of the 1916 Rising among the Nations*, Irish Academic Press, Dublin, 2008.
O'Faolain, S., *Constance Markievicz*, Cresset Women's Voices, London, 1987.
O'Farrell, M., 1916, *What the People Saw*, Mercier Press, Cork, 2013.
O'Farrell, M., *50 Things you didn't know about 1916*, Mercier Press, Cork, 2009.
O'Farrell, M., *The 1916 Diaries*, Mercier Press, Cork, 2014.
O'Farrell, P., *Who's Who in the Irish War of Independence and Civil War, 1916-1923*, Lilliput Press, Dublin, 1997.
O'Malley, E., *The Singing Flame*, Mercier Press, Cork, 2012.
Pakenham, T., *The Year of Liberty*, Abacus, London, 2004.
Reeve, C., Reeve, A., *James Connolly and the United States*, Humanities Press, New Jersey, 1978.
Regan, J. M., *Myth and the Irish State*, Irish Academic Press, Kildare, 2013.
Reilly, T., *Joe Stanley, printer to the Rising*, Brandon, Dingle, 2005.
Ring, J., *Erskine Childers, Author of the Riddle of the Sands*, Faber & Faber, London, 2011.
Ryan, G., *The Works, Celebrating 150 Years of Inchicore Works*, (NP), Dublin, 1996.
Ryle Dwyer, T., *Tans, Terror & Troubles, Kerry's Real Fighting Story*, Mercier Press, Cork, 2001.
Shepherd, E., Beesley, G., *Dublin & South Eastern Railway*, Midland Publishing, Leicester, 1998.
Shepherd, E., *The Great Midland Great Western Railway of Ireland: An Illustrated History*, Midland Publishing, Leicester, 1994.
Spindler, K., *Gun Running for Casement*, Collins, London, 1921.
Spindler, K., *The Mystery of the Casement Ship*, Kribe-Verlag, Berlin, 1931.
Stephens, J., *The Insurrection in Dublin*, Maunsel & Co., Dublin and London, 1916.
Stiles, D., *Portrait of a Rebellion*, CreateSpace Independent Publishing, 2012
Sweeney, P., *Liffey Ships & Shipbuilding*, Mercier Press, Cork, 2010.
Willoughby, R., *A Military History of the University of Dublin and its OTC*, Medal Society of Ireland, Dublin, 1989.
Wills, C., *Dublin 1916*, Profile Books, London, 2009.
Yeates, P., *A City in Wartime, Dublin 1914-18*, Gill & Macmillan, Dublin, 2011.
Yeates, P., *Lockout, Dublin 1913*, Gill & Macmillan, Dublin, 2013.
Younger, C., *Arthur Griffith*, Gill & Macmillan, Dublin, 1981.

# Glossary

| | |
|---|---|
| **Act of Union** | This came into effect on 1st January 1801 and united the kingdoms of Great Britain and Ireland, thus creating the 'United Kingdom of Great Britain and Ireland'. |
| **ADC** | *Aide de Camp.* |
| **Amiens Street Railway Station** | Opened in 1844, renamed Connolly Station in 1966. |
| **Arbour Hill Detention Barracks** | Now a civilian prison. The graveyard at the rear, where the 1916 leaders are buried, is now a public space. |
| ***Ardfheis*** | National convention. |
| ***Bocage*** | Terrain of hedgerows, trees and fields, as in Normandy in France – and in County Meath. |
| **Catholic Emancipation** | This generally refers to the enactment of the Roman Catholic Relief Act in 1829, which abolished the remaining Penal Laws. It was achieved principally through the efforts of Daniel O'Connell's Catholic Association. |
| ***An Claidheamh Soluis*** | The sword of light, a legendary Irish weapon. |
| ***Cumann na mBan*** | Founded in early 1914, this republican women's auxiliary corps supported the objectives of the Irish Volunteers. *Cumann na mBan* participated strongly during the Rising as an active, but noncombatant, support organisation. |
| **Commandant** | A military rank used in Ireland, equivalent to 'Major' in some other armies. |
| **Curragh Camp** | The Curragh has been a place of military assembly on the flat plains of County Kildare for centuries. In the early years of the 20th century it was the principal base of the British Army in Ireland. It is now the main training centre for the Irish Defence Forces. |
| **D&SER** | Dublin & South Eastern Railway. |
| **DBC** | Dublin Bread Company restaurant, 6 &7, Lower Sackville Street. Totally destroyed during Easter Week. |
| **Dissenter** | Presbyterian – not willing to be bound by the Act of Uniformity. |
| **DMP** | Dublin Metropolitan Police. An unarmed urban police force in Dublin, merged into the Garda Síochána in 1925. The G Division (its detectives were popularly known as 'G-men') was a plain-clothes section which gathered intelligence on Irish republicanism dating back to the time of the Fenians. |
| **Fenianism** | A revolutionary movement, originating in the new Irish immigrant population of the USA in the mid-19th century. Its objective was the establishment of an independent Irish Republic. See 'IRB'. |
| ***Fianna Éireann*** | Irish nationalist youth organisation founded by Countess Markievicz and Bulmer Hobson in 1909. |
| **Free State** | The state (known as the Irish Free State or in Irish *Saorstát Éireann*), a self-governing dominion of the British Empire, established on 6 December 1922 under the terms of the Anglo-Irish Treaty, replacing the (transitional) Provisional Government established in January 1922. Its remit covered 26 counties of Ireland. |
| **GAA** | Gaelic Athletic Association. Founded in 1884, a sporting and cultural organisation, which focuses on promoting and organising Gaelic games. |
| **Gaelic League** | Founded in 1893, to promote the Irish language. (in Irish: *Conradh na Gaelige.*) |
| **GNR (I)** | Great Northern Railway (Ireland). |
| **GOC** | General Officer Commanding. |
| **GPO** | General Post Office, on the western side of Lower (formerly Sackville) O'Connell Street in Dublin. An imposingly large building, headquarters of the Irish Post Office. The republican forces seized this and set up their headquarters here during Easter 1916. |
| **GR** | A home defence force in Dublin during 1916, styled Georgius Rex (King George), mainly composed of older men. |
| **Grand Canal** | The more southerly of the two canals that connect Dublin to the Shannon river in the west. The original main line ran to Grand Canal Harbour near St James's Gate in Dublin (now filled in, most of its length is used by a Luas light rail line).The Grand Canal is still in place in Dublin: from the west of the city via Crumlin and Rathmines to where it joins the Liffey at Ringsend. |
| **Great Brunswick Street** | Renamed Pearse Street, after Patrick Pearse. |
| **The Great Famine** | Famines in the period 1845 to 1849 arising from the failure of the potato crop, staple diet of the rural masses. |
| **GS&WR** | Great Southern & Western Railway. |
| **Home Rule** | The aim of 'Home Rule' had as its aim the establishment of a parliament and government in Dublin to legislate for Irish domestic affairs, thus repatriating some aspects of government back from Westminster. |
| **ICA** | Irish Citizen Army. It was founded in November 1913 as a workers' defence militia, following the brutal tactics of the police during the labour rallies led by James Larkin during the 1913 Lockout. After Larkin's departure to the USA, it was organised and directed by James Connolly. The ICA participated strongly in the Rising. |

| | |
|---|---|
| **INV** | Irish National Volunteers. This was the name adopted by the Volunteers who sided with John Redmond in 1914. Many joined the British Army and fought in the war, but the majority of the Irish National Volunteers did not. |
| **Irish Parliamentary Party** | It was formed in 1882 by Charles Stewart Parnell. Its MPs promoted three Home Rule Bills. After the split over Parnell, John Redmond emerged as its leader. The 1918 general election was disastrous for the party and it was dissolved. |
| **IRA** | Irish Republican Army, which had its origins in the Irish Volunteers established in November 1913. During Easter 1916, as the ICA and Irish Volunteers fought together as a combined force, James Connolly used the term 'Irish Republican Army'. It is a title that has had many claimants over the past century. |
| **IRB** | Irish Republican Brotherhood. A secret oath-bound society, prepared to use force to establish an independent Irish Republic, which represented the continuation of the Fenian tradition. The organisation dissolved itself in 1924. |
| **Irish Volunteers** | A nationalist militia founded in November 1913 at the Rotunda in Dublin to 'secure the rights and liberties common to all the people of Ireland'. After the outbreak of WW I in 1914, as the Redmond majority departed with the objective of supporting the British war effort, the remainder of radical nationalists, effectively under IRB, reorganised and made plans for a rising. |
| **ITGWU** | Irish Transport and General Workers' Union, founded by James Larkin in 1909. |
| **Kilmainham Gaol** | Dating from 1796, this grim institution was finally decommissioned as a prison in 1924. Now one of Ireland's top historical sites, with exhibits and tours. |
| **Kingsbridge Railway Station** | Opened in 1846, renamed Heuston Station in 1966 – fittingly after Seán Heuston who worked there for the GS&WR. |
| **Kingstown** | Renamed Dún Laoghaire. |
| **LNWR** | London and North Western Railway. |
| **Marlborough Barracks, Blackhorse Avenue** | Renamed McKee Barracks, still an operational barracks of the Irish Defence Forces. |
| **MGWR** | Midland Great Western Railway. |
| **MP** | Member of Parliament. |
| **OTC** | Officer Training Corps |
| **Penal Laws** | A series of laws enacted from the 1690s which restricted Dissenters and principally Catholics in Ireland, in an effort to promote the established church and to establish dominance over the native Irish. |
| **Portobello Barracks, Rathmines** | Renamed Cathal Brugha Barracks, still an operational barracks of the Irish Defence Forces. |
| **Queenstown** | Renamed Cobh. |
| **RCSI** | Royal College of Surgeons in Ireland. A medical training institution (a recognised college of the National University of Ireland), located on St. Stephen's Green and dating back to 1784. |
| **RIC** | Royal Irish Constabulary, an armed police force in Ireland (outside of Dublin), in existence up to 1922. |
| **Richmond Barracks, Inchicore** | Renamed Keogh Barracks. Since demolished except for a few buildings including the historic gymnasium (which housed republican prisoners after the Rising), now being refurbished to open as a visitor centre. |
| **Royal Barracks, Benburb Street** | Renamed Collins Barracks. Now home to the National Museum of Ireland, Decorative Arts and History. |
| **Sackville Street** | Renamed O'Connell Street. |
| **SDU** | South Dublin Union, with main entrance on James's Street. In 1916 it was a large complex of buildings (hospitals, asylums, convents, churches and ancillary buildings) on 20 hectares. The site now accommodates St James's Hospital. |
| ***Sinn Féin*** | Founded in 1905, under the leadership of Arthur Griffith, who wished to establish a national legislature in Ireland. Griffith and the organisation did not participate in the Rising despite it being dubbed the 'Sinn Féin Rising'. It was restructured in 1917 to take a more radical nationalist and republican direction. |
| **Society of United Irishmen** | Formed in 1791, this non-sectarian radical organisation was inspired by the French and American revolutions. It had the objective of establishing a sovereign, independent Irish Republic. It was central to the rebellion of 1798. |
| **TCD** | Trinity College, Dublin or, in full, 'the College of the Holy and Undivided Trinity of Queen Elizabeth', the sole constituent college of the University of Dublin, founded in 1592. |
| **The O'Rahilly** | Michael Joseph O'Rahilly. A founding member of the Irish Volunteers. 'The' signifies the head of the O'Rahilly clan. |
| **Unionism** | In the Irish context, it is an ideology which supports political union between Ireland and Great Britain. |
| **UVF** | Ulster Volunteer Force. Founded in January 1913, it was a unionist militia, based in Ulster, with the objective of blocking Home Rule in Ireland. |
| **Westland Row Railway Station** | The first railway terminus in Dublin (1834), renamed Pearse Station in 1966. |

# Index